European Cooperation in Higher Education

European Cooperation in Higher Education: Shaping the Future of Europe

BY

IRYNA KUSHNIR
Nottingham Trent University, UK

WITH

NUVE YAZGAN
Nottingham Trent University, UK

United Kingdom – North America – Japan – India – Malaysia – China

Emerald Publishing Limited
Emerald Publishing, Floor 5, Northspring, 21-23 Wellington Street, Leeds LS1 4DL

First edition 2025

Copyright © 2025 Iryna Kushnir.
Chapters 2, 5 and 6 © 2025 Iryna Kushnir and Nuve Yazgan.
Published by Emerald Publishing Limited.

 The ebook edition of this title is Open Access and is freely available to read online.

This work is published under the Creative Commons Attribution (CC BY 4.0) licence. Anyone may reproduce, distribute, translate and create derivative works of this book (for both commercial and non-commercial purposes), subject to full attribution to the original publication and authors. The full terms of this licence may be seen at http://creativecommons.org/licences/by/4.0/legalcode

British Library Cataloguing in Publication Data
A catalogue record for this book is available from the British Library

ISBN: 978-1-83753-519-4 (Print)
ISBN: 978-1-83753-516-3 (Online)
ISBN: 978-1-83753-518-7 (Epub)

INVESTOR IN PEOPLE

This book is dedicated to my K., the miracle.

Contents

List of Vignettes	*ix*
List of Tables	*xi*
List of Abbreviations	*xiii*
About the Author	*xv*
About the Contributor	*xvii*
Preface	*xix*
Acknowledgements	*xxi*

Chapter 1   Introduction *1*
Iryna Kushnir

Chapter 2   The Neo-Institutionalist Approach *17*
Iryna Kushnir and Nuve Yazgan

Chapter 3   The European Project and European Higher Education *31*
Iryna Kushnir

Chapter 4   Germany's Membership in the European Higher Education Area: Leading Europe *45*
Iryna Kushnir

Chapter 5   France's Membership in the European Higher Education Area: (Still) 'Moderating' the Leading of Europe *57*
Iryna Kushnir and Nuve Yazgan

Chapter 6 Italy's Membership in the European Higher Education Area: Coordinating Cooperation in Higher Education While Attempting to Stay Apolitical   *73*
Iryna Kushnir and Nuve Yazgan

Chapter 7 United Kingdom's Membership(s) in the European Higher Education Area: Applying a Heterogeneous Agenda   *89*
Iryna Kushnir

Chapter 8 European Cooperation in Higher Education and the Evolving Mission of the European Project (in the Early 2020s)   *107*
Iryna Kushnir

Chapter 9 Conclusion   *121*
Iryna Kushnir

Index   *129*

List of Vignettes

Chapter 1
Vignette 1. List of EHEA International Official
             Communications.   12

List of Tables

Chapter 1

Table 1.	Stakeholders in the United Kingdom (EWNI and Scotland), Germany, France and Italy.	7
Table 2.	List of Interviewees.	9
Table 3.	Official Communications From National Stakeholders.	11

List of Abbreviations

ADIUT	The Assembly of Directors of University Institutes of Technology in France
AfD	German Alternative for Germany
ALFA	The América Latina – Formación Académica programme
ANVUR	Italian Quality Assurance Agency
BERA	British Educational Research Association
BFUG	Bologna Follow-up Group
BP	Bologna Process
CAS	Common Asylum System
CRUI	The Conference of Italian University Rectors
DAAD	German Academic Exchange Service
EC	European Commission
ECTS	European Credit Transfer System
EEA	European Education Area
EHEA	European Higher Education Area
ENIC	The European Network of Information Centres
ERASMUS	European Community Action Scheme for the Mobility of University Students
ET	Education and Training
EU	European Union
EWNI	England, Wales and Northern Ireland
FAGE	National Student Organisation in France
FdI	Brothers of Italy
FI	Forza Italia
FZS	Free Association of Students' Unions in Germany
GEW	Education and Science Workers' Union in Germany
HE	Higher Education
M5s	The Five Star Movement in Italy

MSs	Member States (of the EU)
NARIC	National Academic Recognition Information Centres (in the European Union)
NATO	The North Atlantic Treaty Organisation
NI	New institutionalism
NUS	National Union of Students in the UK
PD	The Democratic Party Partito Democraticoarty in Italy
PdL	Il Popolo della Libertà (the People of Freedom party in Italy)
QAC	The Quality Assurance Committee (in Italy)
UDU	National Union of University Students in Italy
UK	United Kingdom
WWII	Second World War

About the Author

Iryna Kushnir is the author of this book. She is an Associate Professor at the Nottingham Institute of Education at Nottingham Trent University. Prior to this, she held academic posts at the University of Edinburgh and the University of Sheffield. Dr Kushnir's interdisciplinary research combines the following main areas: higher education policy and sociology, European integration and social justice. She is particularly interested, and has published widely, in the area of higher education policy and politics of the European Higher Education Area. She was the PI on the project which laid the foundation for this book. This project was funded by the Spencer Foundation and was entitled 'Europeanisation agenda and membership in the European Higher Education Area post-2020: stakeholders' perspectives from the UK, Germany, France and Italy'. Dr Kushnir's interdisciplinary approach has led to empirical and theoretical contributions, which reveal how education policy on one hand and Europeanisation processes on the other hand are interrelated and mutually shape one another. A wider societal impact of Dr Kushnir's work is in co-establishing and co-developing the Ukrainian Education Research Association which has become the biggest national research association in Ukraine and a hub for education research and quality.

About the Contributor

Nuve Yazgan has co-authored three of the nine chapters in this book together with Dr Iryna Kushnir (Chapters 2, 5 and 6). Dr Nuve Yazgan has worked as a Research Consultant at Full Fact as well as a researcher at the Nottingham Institute of Education at Nottingham Trent University and at the Department of Government at the University of Essex. During her time at Nottingham Trent University, she was employed by Dr Iryna Kushnir to contribute to some aspects of the project which are presented in this book. Dr Yazgan completed her PhD studies in December 2021 at the Department of Politics at the University of Surrey. Her research interests include European Public Policy, Greek Politics and Greek–Turkish Relations. She has published articles and book reviews in various journals.

Preface

This book explores the role of European cooperation in higher education (HE), illustrated by the case of the European Higher Education Area (EHEA), in understanding the evolving mission of the European project that has increasingly been transcending the borders of the European Union. The temporal focus of this book is on the early 2020s, but relevant developments prior to this are also considered as an important context.

The focus of this book is timely and original, first of all, because the book reports on the only study about the four founders of the EHEA, focusing on the interconnectedness of their EHEA membership agendas and their wider political agendas. Second, the study reported here addresses a temporal-contextual gap in the available field of research on the EHEA by covering the early 2020s period, namely after the last 2020 deadline for the development of the EHEA, as well as after such significant political events in the European region as the end of the Brexit transitional period and the start of a full-scale Russia–Ukraine war. Third, the study presented in this book highlights an innovative theoretical dimension in the topic of European HE and European politics by relying on neo-institutionalism.

The analysis in this book is informed by neo-institutionalism and relies on 25 interviews with key policy actors in the four founding countries of the EHEA (i.e., Germany, France, Italy and the United Kingdom) and text analysis of 64 selected official communications. Through an in-depth examination of the generated empirical data in light of the underlying theory and prior studies in the area of European HE and politics, this book aims to (1) explore the perspectives of key HE actors in the four founding countries of the EHEA on the strategic significance of their memberships in this area for them, as well as for the European region, and (2) analyse these findings to inform our understanding of the evolving mission of the European project.

The significance of the analysis in this book is in demonstrating that European cooperation in HE, exemplified by the EHEA, has been a platform for the meaning-making process of the European project's mission which has been gaining momentum in supporting political stability in the European region, predominantly recently – post-2020. The findings presented in this book suggest that the stakeholders of each of the EHEA's founding countries, despite having different priorities and visions for their memberships in the EHEA and EHEA's role for Europe, have all been contributory to the making of the purpose of the European project as an insurer of stability and dialogue among the countries.

Based on these findings, the study presented in this book addresses gaps in the literature on European HE and the European project and informs policy practice at the EHEA international policymaking level in the run-up to EHEA's 2030 deadline, the national policymaking level of the four EHEA founders in the area of HE and international relations, as well as further work of the European Commission and its partners in steering the development of the European project.

Acknowledgements

I would like to express my gratitude to my interview participants for sharing their valuable expertise and insights.

Special thanks should also go to the research funders whose support laid the foundation for this important book. The research reported in this book was made possible (in part) by a grant from the Spencer Foundation (#202200185) and funding from Research England, awarded through Nottingham Trent University, granted to Dr Iryna Kushnir. The views expressed are those of the author and do not necessarily reflect the views of the funders.

I would like to acknowledge the loving and inspiring support of my husband, family, friends and colleagues.

Chapter 1

Introduction

Authored by Iryna Kushnir

Abstract

This opening chapter contextualises the focus of the book, explains its originality, and outlines the research design of the project which is reported in this book. Special attention is paid to the collective case study of the four countries that inform the empirical part of this study: Germany, France, Italy and the United Kingdom, as members and founders of the European Higher Education Area. Data collection and analysis methods are also detailed here.

Keywords: Europe; the European project; politics; Europeanisation; European Higher Education Area; higher education; UK; Germany; France; Italy

1.1 Background and Relevance: Europe, its Higher Education and the European Higher Education Area

Post-WWII peace-building and the promotion of security assurance on the European continent became the main impetus to the emergence of the European Union (EU) and its development, with the collapse of the Soviet Union and Yugoslavia in 1991 adding fuel to that aspiration (Dedman, 2009). The signing of the Maastricht Treaty in 1992 and its ratification in 1993 formally established the EU, with an initial membership of 12 countries, and commenced a new stage in the development of a so-called European project, the territorial reach and meaning of which have evolved over time (EU, 2024). While the borders of the EU have been a matter of political agreements, the European project has been developing as a space of meaning, that increasingly transcends the borders of the EU and aims to unite Europe as a region the geography of which spans beyond EU's borders (Kushnir, 2016). Hence, Europeanisation has been the accompanying process of the evolution of the European project, and its dynamic nature could be understood as a process of adopting the aims and features to support the development of the European project (Exadaktylos et al., 2020).

The establishment of the post-1945 European institutions largely aimed to make another war in the European area politically unthinkable and materially not possible. Nonetheless, those post-war institutions ended up prioritising elite governance over popular participation. As a result, a Europe founded on education seems to have started appearing as a more truly people's Europe than what we have inherited from the post-1945 institutions. Education has emerged as an instrument for defeating a lack of unity within the EU, and even more so, for developing deeper relationships between the EU member states, as well as between the EU and its neighbours.

Education in general and higher education (HE), in particular, have historically played an important role in European politics. Writing almost two decades ago, Grek (2008, p. 208) argued that education was 'slowly moving from the margins of European governance to the very centre of its policy making.' More recently, I have emphasised a similar phenomenon in my paper (Kushnir, 2021b), highlighting how the European Education Area (a related but distinct initiative from the EHEA, meant for all levels of education specifically in the EU countries) has been used by EU decision-makers to facilitate the deepening of the relationships among the EU member states in the context of the rise of populism, economic crises and other challenges the EU has been facing. Robertson et al. (2016) maintain that specifically HE has been instrumental in crafting the European project particularly through facilitating academic mobility, inspiring the building of a European single market and the concept of the European citizen.

The processes that make up the European HE space are complex and have a long history. For example, the EU has been coordinating a number of education policy initiatives with a focus on HE. Examples include the famous Bologna Process (BP) which has established the European Higher Education Area (EHEA) and the associated Education and Training (ET) Work frameworks 2010/2020, which both later served as a foundation for the European Education Area (Robertson et al., 2022). Feeding on these growing policy interconnections, the EHEA has emerged as the largest all-encompassing HE harmonisation initiative not only in the European region but much wider – in the world, having transformed into an 'international higher education regime' (Zahavi & Friedman, 2019, p. 23).

Some scholars, seemingly, anticipated or assumed that the work on building the EHEA and its BP would have come to an end back in 2020 (Gareis & Broekel, 2022; Mendick & Peters, 2022; Pires Pereira et al., 2021), which was the deadline for the achievement of a 'fully functioning EHEA' (EHEA, 2024h). However, this did not happen. What follows is a brief reminder about some of the key aspects of the EHEA and its BP.

Education ministers from four countries, namely the United Kingdom, Germany, France and Italy, initiated work towards the EHEA at their meeting in France in 1998, before calling upon other EU member states to join them (EHEA, 2024a). The EHEA started developing as a platform for Europeanisation, more so after the adoption in 2001 of the goal for the EU to become 'the most competitive and dynamic knowledge-based economy in the world.' This followed Lisbon

Council in 2000 when this goal was originally set specifically for the EU (Corbett, 2011, p. 36). The link of the EHEA and Europeanisation was reinforced by EHEA's growing membership initially limited to the EU countries, frequent references in the EHEA official communications to developing a European identity of those in the EHEA and, after all, the inclusion of the term 'European' in the actual name of the EHEA (Kushnir, 2016). Eventually, the EHEA started broadening European borders by inviting non-EU countries to become members, but this was accompanied 'by aggravating tensions in the development of a territory-identity integrity in Europe, constructed by the Bologna Process' (Kushnir, 2016, p. 665). Nonetheless, the BP has grown to become the biggest HE initiative worldwide (Zahavi & Friedman, 2019).

The BP has evolved over time. Initially, it was about harmonising HE systems in the EHEA to ease academic mobility and employability (e.g. comparable cycles of studies, credit system to measure workload, quality assurance standards, etc.) (EHEA, 2024a). Then, the focus was more on developing and implementing the values of democracy and academic freedom in the EHEA, as suggested by the Rome Ministerial Communique (EHEA, 2020). More recently, in the context of the Russian full-scale invasion of Ukraine, 'the EHEA has begun to emerge as a platform for political cooperation beyond HE for the promotion of peace in the European region' (Kushnir, 2023, p. 1). Not only did the scope of the Bologna initiatives evolve, but so did the territorial reach of the EHEA. Currently, there are 47 active members in the EHEA, following the suspension of the memberships of Russia and Belarus in April 2022 in response to the invasion of Ukraine (EHEA, 2022).

This brings us back to reasoning about the mission of Europe. The peace-promotion ideal, mentioned above, gradually became a thing of the past, as new generations could not relate to it. Polyakova's (2016, p. 70) powerful words shed more light on this,

> Mainstream politicians too often rely on the worn-out trope of a Europe "whole, free, and at peace" – a phrase that spoke to generations that remembered World War II and the Cold War. But younger Europeans are searching for a vision for the future that speaks to their values now, not to ideals that emerged out of past calamities.

Nevertheless, as the findings spelled out later in this book will demonstrate, Polyakova's (2016) observation has begun to change with the start of the full-scale invasion of Ukraine, evidenced by the case of the EHEA. This is one key aspects of the relationship between European cooperation in HE and the evolving mission of Europe that will be discussed in this book.

1.2 The Focus and Originality of This Book

This book explores the role of European cooperation in HE, illustrated by cooperation in the framework of the EHEA, in understanding the evolving mission of the

European project in the early 2020s. This focus of the book is timely and original for three main reasons. First, this book reports on the only study about the four founders of the EHEA, focusing on the interconnectedness of their EHEA membership agendas and their wider political agendas. Second, the study reported here addresses a temporal-contextual gap in the available field of research on the EHEA by covering the most recent period of the early 2020s, namely after the Brexit transitional period and after the start of a full-scale Russia–Ukraine war. Third, the study highlights an innovative theoretical dimension in this topic – relying on neo-institutionalism in the analysis of Europeanisation politics particularly in the context of EHEA memberships.

While the literature about the participation of Germany, France, Italy and the United Kingdom in the EHEA is diverse, no research explores them jointly as the four founders of the EHEA, with the exception of my recent co-authored article on the geopolitics of the European HE space (Kushnir & Yazgan, 2024) that stems from this same project and represents its extract. Part of the significance of this book lies in addressing this gap by investigating the role of European cooperation in HE represented by the EHEA in understanding the evolving mission of the European project.

This first collective case study makes an essential contribution to the scholarship about the EHEA by advancing our limited knowledge about its initiators and their Europeanisation in the early 2020s. Revealing these trends is also significant and timely for theorising differentiated Europeanisation from a HE perspective and informing EHEA international level policymaking in the run-up to its new deadline of 2030. The first years after the 19 November, 2020 stocktaking ministerial meeting are crucial in shaping the directions of work of EHEA's signatories. Although the concept 'differentiated Europeanisation' stems from EU Studies, it has also been applied to the analysis of the EHEA, the boundaries of which spread far beyond the EU. Veiga et al. (2015) applied it, but only in the area of HE harmonisation and only in the context of Germany, Italy, Norway and Portugal. Even though Germany and Italy featured in that study, it did not answer the questions posed by the project reported in this book. This is because the scholars relied only on the analysis of country's Bologna reports prior to 2009, did not review the situation post-2020, did not offer an in-depth exploration of the perspectives of key HE actors on the EHEA membership and did not view it as a case of a wider Europeanisation agenda of the countries. Veiga's (2023) more recent reflective piece brings together the discussion of political differentiated integration in the EU and differences within the EHEA. While discussing Brexit, this work does not specifically focus on the temporal context of the early 2020s and the full-scale invasion of Ukraine. It also does not rely on empirical research, which means it does not focus on data collected from the stakeholders in the four founders of the EHEA and does not apply the neo-institutionalist lens.

There is a need to bridge the scholarship about EHEA membership and wider Europeanisation particularly with regard to the countries that initiated the EHEA – as a platform for Europeanisation to understand the nature of this Europeanisation. The state of affairs in the early 2020s is of a special interest here because in addition to the change of European geopolitics in 2020 following the end of Brexit transitional period, the year 2020 was the deadline for the achievement of a 'fully-functioning EHEA' (EHEA, 2024h) and planning EHEA's further work.

In light of the above, the specific research questions that this book sets out to explore include:

> What is the role of European cooperation in HE represented by the EHEA for the evolving mission of the European project in the early 2020s?
>
> (1) What are the perspectives of key HE actors in the four founding countries of the EHEA (Germany, France, Italy and the UK) on the strategic significance of their memberships in this Area for them, as well as for the European region?
> (2) How do these findings inform our understanding of the European project?

By exploring the answers to the above research questions, this book puts forward and unfolds the following argument: European cooperation in HE, illustrated here by the case of the EHEA, is an instrumental platform for the meaning-making process of the European project's mission which has increasingly been gaining momentum in supporting political stability in the European region, particularly in the early 2020s period. The findings suggest that the stakeholders of each of the EHEA's founders, despite having different priorities and visions for their memberships in the EHEA and EHEA's role for Europe, have all been contributing to the crafting of the purpose of the European project, that has increasingly been transcending the borders of the EU, as an insurer of stability and cross-country dialogue.

Specifically, German Bologna stakeholders view Germany's EHEA membership largely as a tool for generating and maintaining political stability in the region, and Germany takes an active leading role in this process. France's Bologna stakeholders take a moderating role in leading the European region together with Germany in their stability-seeking process relying on the EHEA as a platform for this. Italian EHEA-related stakeholders, despite taking a coordinating role in the EHEA, have been trialling ways of staying apolitical before succumbing to the unavoidable connection between politics and HE. This attitude to politics may, arguably, be rooted predominantly in the assumed conflict between EHEA's inherent link to Europeanisation (Kushnir, 2021a) and Italy's growing Euroscepticism, coupled with a commitment to the security of the region. A similar conflict seems to be present in the attitude of England, Wales and N. Ireland (EWNI) which is one of the two UK members in the EHEA, along with Scotland, but this conflict is expressed differently in EWNI's positioning of its EHEA membership. EWNI, where England's Bologna stakeholders set the tone for work (Kushnir & Brooks, 2022), have been focused on observing the developments in the EHEA and wider politics surrounding it, keeping the HE cooperation ties which have been established and looking outwards to cooperating with other regions. EWNI's attitude to the Europeanisation politics of the European region is that of a former empire – willingness to maintain international connections and external influence, while not being an active leader in the EHEA or in the European project. For Scotland, which is the other UK member in the EHEA, HE cooperation in the framework of the EHEA is an instrument for Scotland's politics of Europeanisation, particularly the mending of the EU ties, shaken after Brexit.

1.3 A Note on the Memberships of the United Kingdom, Germany, France and Italy in the European Higher Education Area

The first striking difference regarding the membership status of the four cases in the EHEA is that unlike the other three cases, the United Kingdom has two separate 'seats' – for Scotland and separately for England, Wales and Northern Ireland (EWNI). The United Kingdom's two memberships are presented on the EHEA website as the 'United Kingdom', which refers to EWNI, and the 'United Kingdom (Scotland)' which stands only for Scotland (EHEA, 2024b). Aside from this, it is also important to point out that Germany's membership has its own complexity, given Germany's federal states' independence in policymaking (Toens, 2009).

UK-devolved administrations and their related policy actors work together in governing HE in different parts of the United Kingdom (Gallacher & Raffe, 2012), and thus, tight links and some overlaps in the work of key stakeholders from EWNI and Scotland were considered. Evidently, the list of German, French and Italian stakeholders in the EHEA is less complex, given their singular membership in the EHEA (Table 1).

1.4 Methodological Considerations

The overarching research design of this project was informed by BERA (2018) Research Ethics Guidelines, which was the latest edition of the Guidelines at the time of designing this project. Data collection followed a favourable ethics decision (Ref: KUSHNIR 2021/414) from the Schools of Business, Law and Social Sciences Research Ethics Committee (BLSS REC) at Nottingham Trent University. The write-up of this book is also informed by relevant updates in the recently published fifth edition of the BERA (2024) Research Ethics Guidelines.

This book presents a collective case study of four EHEA's founders' perspectives on the role of European cooperation in HE represented by the EHEA in the evolving mission of the European project in the early 2020s.[1] As per Stake's (1994) definition, a collective case study involves some level of comparison, but it

---

[1] The research reported in this book was made possible (in part) by a grant from the Spencer Foundation (#202200185) as well as Research England, awarded through Nottingham Trent University to Dr Iryna Kushnir. The views expressed are those of the authors and do not necessarily reflect the views of the funders.

Table 1. Stakeholders in the United Kingdom (EWNI and Scotland), Germany, France and Italy.

Stakeholders	UK (EWNI)	UK (Scotland)	Germany	France	Italy
1. National Authority for HE	Department for Education (Government)	Scottish Government	Federal Ministry of Education and Research	Ministry of Higher Education, Research and Innovation	Ministry of Education and Merit
2. Quality Assurance Authority	Quality Assurance Agency	Quality Assurance Agency Scotland	Accreditation Council	High Council for the Evaluation of Research and Higher Education	National Agency for the Evaluation of the University and Research System (ANVUR)
3. Student Unions	National Union of Students (NUS-UK)	National Union of Students Scotland (NUS-Scotland)	National Union of Students in Germany	National Union of Students in France (UNEF) European Students Union (FAGE)	National Council of University Students
4. Employers' Associations/ Teachers Unions	University and College Union	University College Union Scotland	Confederation of German Employers' Association Education and Science Workers' Union (GEW)	Mouvement des Entreprises de France (MEDEF)	—

(Continued)

Table 1. (Continued)

Stakeholders	UK (EWNI)	UK (Scotland)	Germany	France	Italy
5. Recognised National HE Organisations	Guild HE Universities UK Association of Colleges	Universities Scotland Colleges Scotland	—	National Higher Institutions Conference	Conference of Directors-General of University Administrations
6. National Qualifications Body	Qualification and Credit Framework for England, Wales and Northern Ireland	Scottish Credit and Qualifications Framework	—	National Commission for Vocational Certification	Italian Qualifications Framework for Higher education
7. Rectors Associations	—	—	Rectors' Conference	National Rectors' Conference	Conference of Rectors of Italian Universities (CRIU)
8. Academic Recognition Body	NARIC UK		ENIC-NARIC Germany	ENIC-NARIC France	ENIC-NARIC Italy
9. EU Education Programmes	Erasmus+ National Agency International Credit Mobility		Erasmus+ National Contact Point	Agence Erasmus+ France/Education Formation	Erasmus+ National Contact Point
10. Information Agency for International Students and Scholars	—	—	German Academic Exchange Service (DAAD)	Agence Campus France	Academic Equivalence Mobility Information Centre (CIMEA) UNIVERSITALY

Source: Based on the information provided on the EHEA website (EHEA, 2024c, 2024d, 2024e, 2024f, 2024g).

is not a comparative study per se. Instead, it aims to provide a comprehensive discussion of the issue under investigation across several cases. The analysis in this book relies on (1) in-depth semi-structured elite interviews with an opportunistic/snowball sample of key Bologna stakeholders in the countries of interest, as well as (2) their official communications, both on the national as well as the international level of the EHEA.[2]

The interviews (see Table 2) with EHEA stakeholders in the four countries (Germany $n = 8$, France $n = 4$, Italy $n = 7$, UK $n = 6$) were conducted in 2022, except for the UK case study. The interviews in the United Kingdom were conducted in 2021, as the first phase of the project. While the timing of the UK interviews (January–March 2021) – a few months earlier than the rest of the interviews (January–July 2022) – did not seem to have an impact on the content of what was discussed, there was one important topic that was omitted from the UK interviews because of their timing. The fact that they took place a few months before the launch of the full-scale attack on Ukraine by Russia in February 2022 meant that the UK stakeholders' responses to the war were not a matter of discussion.

Table 2. List of Interviewees.

Case Study	Interviewee's Codes and Affiliations (Unless Interviewees Requested to Represent Their Affiliation as a 'Key HE Actor')
UK	A1. Guild HE (England, Wales, N. Ireland and Scotland)
	A2. Key HE actor in the UK (Scotland)
	A3. National Union of Students (NUS-UK) (England, Wales, N. Ireland)
	A4. Scottish Government (Scotland)
	A5. Universities UK International (England, Wales, N. Ireland)
	A6. National Union of Students (NUS-Scotland) (Scotland)
Germany	B1. Federal Ministry of education and Research
	B2. Key HE actor
	B3. Key HE actor
	B4. Rectors' Conference
	B5. Free association of students' unions (FZS)
	B6. Erasmus+ National Agency, DAAD
	B7. Key HE actor
	B8. Education and Science Workers' Union (GEW)

(Continued)

---

[2]The dataset with interview transcripts, generated and analysed during the research project that informs this book, is available in the Research Data Archive of Nottingham Trent University, at https://doi.org/10.17631/RD-2022-0001-DDOC.

Table 2. *(Continued)*

Case Study	Interviewee's Codes and Affiliations (Unless Interviewees Requested to Represent Their Affiliation as a 'Key HE Actor')
France	C1. Representative from ENIC-NARIC France
	C2. French expert in the Bologna Process
	C3. Representative of the Assembly of Directors of University Institutes of Technology (ADIUT)
	C4. Representative of a national student organisation (FAGE)
Italy	D1. Key HE actor
	D2. Key HE actor
	D3. Representative of the Italian quality assurance agency (ANVUR)
	D4. Key HE actor
	D5. Representative of the National Union of University Students (UDU)
	D6. Former vice-chair of the Bologna Follow-up Group in Italy
	D7. Representative of the Conference of Italian University Rectors (CRUI)

The participants for the interviews were initially recruited through contact information on key HE stakeholders' websites, provided on the EHEA website, and subsequent contacts that followed. Each interview lasted about an hour and, being informed by the neo-institutionalist approach, focused on strategic decisions of these stakeholders regarding their work in the EHEA and the implications it has had for Europe.

In order to bolster the claims made by the interviewees, supplementary data were sought from the official communications, both on the national levels of the countries of interest, as well as the international level of the EHEA. Some national official communications were provided by the interviewees, other official communications were searched on the stakeholders' websites (Table 1) of each of the four countries, using the keywords 'Bologna', 'European Higher Education Area', 'EHEA', 'European Union', 'EU', 'Europe', 'European' and 'Brexit'. For some of the Bologna actors listed on the EHEA website, the search did not return any results (EHEA, 2024c, 2024d, 2024e; 2024f, 2024g). This may be either due to their more passive involvement in the reforms, as some of them also suggested in their e-mail responses to the invitations for interviews or due to being guided by more centrally issued documents, such as by relevant ministries. Table 3 below provides the list of the stakeholders whose official communications have been analysed and the number of these official communications that was sourced.

Acknowledging that both the interview data and national-level official communications prioritise the views of a few EHEA actors, international official

Table 3. Official Communications From National Stakeholders.

Number of Official Communications Analysed per Stakeholder			Total Number per Case Study
From UK stakeholders	Central Government (EWNI and Scotland)	4	19
	Quality Assurance Agency (EWNI and Scotland)	1	
	Universities UK International (EWNI and Scotland)	12	
	Association of Colleges (EWNI and Scotland)	1	
	Universities Scotland (Scotland)	1	
From German stakeholders	Federal government	6	10
	Federal government's advisory body (German Science and Humanities Council)	1	
	Rectors' Conference	2	
	Collaborative report (federal government, Rectors' Conference, DAAD, FZS, Accreditation Council, DSW, GEW, BDA)	1	
From French stakeholders	Ministry of Higher education, Research and Innovation	22	25
	High Council for the Evaluation of Research and Higher Education	1	
	Free Association of Students' Unions (FAGE)	2	
From Italian stakeholders	Italian Quality Assurance Agency (ANVUR)	2	10
	National Union of University Students (UDU)	4	
	Representative of the Conference of Italian University Rectors (CRUI)	1	
	Ministry of Education and Merit	1	
	ENIC-NARIC Italy	2	

communications were included to consider the significant roles of other members and consultative members of the EHEA. The international communications that were available on the EHEA website issued between 2016–2022 (Vignette 1) were collected. This time span was chosen because of the 2016 Brexit referendum in the United Kingdom, which intensified the debates about European cooperation after 2016 not only in the United Kingdom but also far beyond in the European region.

> **Vignette 1. List of EHEA International Official Communications.**
>
> EHEA. (2020a). Rome Ministerial Communique. http://www.ehea.info/Upload/Rome_Ministerial_Communique.pdf. Accessed on June 14, 2024.
>
> EHEA. (2020b). Annex I of Rome Ministerial Communique. https://ehea.info/Upload/Rome_Ministerial_Communique_Annex_I.pdf. Accessed on June 14, 2024.
>
> EHEA. (2020c). Annex II of Rome Ministerial Communique. http://www.ehea.info/Upload/Rome_Ministerial_Communique_Annex_II.pdf. Accessed on June 14, 2024.
>
> EHEA. (2020d). Annex III of Rome Ministerial Communique. http://www.ehea.info/Upload/Rome_Ministerial_Communique_Annex_III.pdf. Accessed on June 14, 2024.
>
> EHEA. (2021a). Annex I: Bologna Follow Up Group work plan 2021–2024. http://www.ehea.info/Upload/BFUG_PT_AD_76_5_Work_Plan_and_TORs_Annex_I.pdf. Accessed on June 14, 2024.
>
> EHEA. (2021b). Terms of reference of the working group on global policy dialogue. http://www.ehea.info/Upload/CG_GPD_PT_AD_TORs%20(2).pdf. Accessed on June 14, 2024.
>
> EHEA. (2022a). Draft workplan for discussion at the Coordination Group on Global Policy Dialogue meeting. http://www.ehea.info/Upload/First%20Draft%20Workplan%20CGGPD%5B43977%5D.pdf. Accessed on June 14, 2024.
>
> EHEA. (2022b). Extraordinary BFUG board meeting LXXIX/I. http://ehea.info/Upload/Extraordinary%20Board_FR_AZ_79_1%20minutes%20.pdf. Accessed on June 14, 2024.
>
> EHEA. (2022c). Adoption of the statement by the Bologna Follow-up Group and the suspension of the rights of participation of the Russian Federation and Belarus. http://ehea.info/page-ADOPTION-OF-THE-STATEMENT. Accessed on June 14, 2024.
>
> EHEA. (2022d). Statement by members and consultative members of the Bologna Follow-up Group on consequences of the Russian invasion of Ukraine. http://ehea.info/Upload/STATEMENT%20BY%20MEMBERS%20AND%20CONSULTATIVE%20MEMBERS%20OF%20THE%20BOLOGNA%20FOLLOW%20UP%20GROUP%20ON%20CONSEQUENCES%20OF%20THE%20RUSSIAN%20INVASION%20OF%20UKRAINE.pdf. Accessed on June 14, 2024.

The year 2022 marked the end of the data collection phase for these case studies. The inclusion of these documents adds depth and context to the interviewees' perspectives and allows for a more comprehensive understanding of the issues at hand.

The audio recordings of the interviews were transcribed and then thematically analysed, along with the official communications. The analysis of the interview transcripts and official communications was conducted following Braun and Clarke's (2006) and Clarke and Braun's (2017) framework for analysis, which includes six key phases. Familiarisation and coding – the first two phases – focused on grouping similar data segments. This allowed to identify and take note of the patterns associated with the role of European HE represented by the EHEA in understanding the evolving mission of the European project after 2020. The multiplicity of the codes became the foundation for the next two phases – searching for themes and reviewing them. The remaining two phases focused on defining and naming the themes. Then, the themes were restructured to establish relationships among them and to finalise the super-ordinate themes in an integrated analysis.

Two major themes with important sub-elements were generated: (1) continuing memberships of EHEA founders are a rational-choice of their national Bologna stakeholders interlinked with their countries' wider political stances (i.e. aspiring to lead Europe by Germany though its EHEA membership, supporting and moderating the process of the leading of Europe by France, coordinating the EHEA while (unsuccessfully) trying to stay away from bigger politics by Italy, implementing a heterogenous agenda by the two UK members); (2) the EHEA serving as a platform for the advancement of the meaning of the European project (as a guarantor of stability in the region and international cooperation). Illustrative interview quotations for these themes and their sub-themes were finally supplemented and supported by relevant quotations from the official communications.

1.5 Book Structure

Following this introductory chapter, the book includes subsequent eight chapters.

Chapter 2 provides an underlying theoretical framework for the analysis in this book which revolves around the ideas rooted in neo-institutionalism.

Chapter 3 maps the landscape of existing research on the European project and European cooperation initiatives in higher education, focusing predominantly on the EHEA and points to a few major gaps in this research.

Chapters 4–7 present and discuss the findings generated from the interviews and official communications from Germany, France, Italy and the United Kingdom, respectively, supplemented with the findings from international official communications.

Chapter 8 integrates the findings presented in the four data Chapters 4–7 in light of the theoretical considerations and the literature review presented in Chapters 2–3.

Chapter 9 offers concluding remarks.

References

BERA. (2018). *Ethical guidelines for educational research* (4th ed.). https://www.bera.ac.uk/publication/ethical-guidelines-for-educational-research-2018. Accessed on October 10, 2022.

BERA. (2024). *Ethical guidelines for educational research* (5th ed.). https://www.bera.ac.uk/publication/ethical-guidelines-for-educational-research-fifth-edition-2024. Accessed on June 10, 2024.

Braun, V., & Clarke, V. (2006). Using thematic analysis in psychology. *Qualitative Research in Psychology, 3*(2), 77–101.

Clarke, V., & Braun, V. (2017). Thematic analysis. *The Journal of Positive Psychology, 12*(3), 297–298. https://doi.org/10.1080/17439760.2016.1262613

Corbett, A. (2011). Ping Pong: Competing leadership for reform in EU higher education 1998–2006. *European Journal of Education, 46*(1), 36–53. https://doi.org/10.1111/j.1465-3435.2010.01466.x

Dedman, M. (2009). *The origins & development of the European Union 1945-2008: A history of European integration*. Routledge.

EHEA. (2020). Rome Ministerial Communique. https://ehea.info/Upload/Rome_Ministerial_Communique.pdf. Accessed on February 10, 2025.

EHEA. (2022). Statement by members and consultative members of the Bologna Follow-up Group on consequences of the Russian Federation invasion of Ukraine. http://www.ehea.info/Upload/STATEMENT%20BY%20MEMBERS%20AND%20CONSULTATIVE%20MEMBERS%20OF%20THE%20BOLOGNA%20FOLLOW%20UP%20GROUP%20ON%20CONSEQUENCES%20OF%20THE%20RUSSIAN%20INVASION%20OF%20UKRAINE.pdf. Accessed on September 1, 2024.

EHEA. (2024a). How does the Bologna Process work? https://www.ehea.info/page-how-does-the-bologna-process-work. Accessed on June 10, 2024.

EHEA. (2024b). Full members. https://www.ehea.info/page-full_members. Accessed on June 10, 2024.

EHEA. (2024c). United Kingdom. https://www.ehea.info/page-united-kingdom. Accessed on June 10, 2024.

EHEA. (2024d). Scotland. https://www.ehea.info/page-united-kingdom-scotland. Accessed on June 10, 2024.

EHEA. (2024e). France. https://www.ehea.info/page-france. Accessed on June 10, 2024.

EHEA. (2024f). Germany. https://www.ehea.info/page-germany. Accessed on June 10, 2024.

EHEA. (2024g). Italy. https://www.ehea.info/page-italy. Accessed on June 10, 2024.

EHEA. (2024h). Official website of the European higher education area. https://ehea.info/. Accessed on June 10, 2024.

EU. (2024). History of the EU 1990-1999. https://european-union.europa.eu/principles-countries-history/history-eu/1990-99_en. Accessed on March 29, 2024.

Exadaktylos, T., Graziano, P. R., & Vink, M. P. (2020). *Europeanization: Concept, theory, and methods*. Oxford University Press.

Gallacher, J., & Raffe, D. (2012). Higher education policy in post-devolution UK: More convergence than divergence? *Journal of Education Policy, 27*(4), 467–490. https://doi.org/10.1080/02680939.2011.626080

Gareis, P., & Broekel, T. (2022). The spatial patterns of student mobility before, during and after the Bologna Process in Germany. *Tijdschrift voor Economische en Sociale Geografie*, *113*(3), 290–309. https://doi.org/10.1111/tesg.12507

Grek, S. (2008). From symbols to numbers: The shifting technologies of education governance in Europe. *European Educational Research Journal*, *7*(2), 208–218. https://doi.org/10.2304/eerj.2008.7.2.208

Kushnir, I. (2016). The role of the Bologna Process in defining Europe. *European Educational Research Journal*, *15*(6), 664–675. https://doi.org/10.1177/1474904116657549

Kushnir, I. (2021a). *The Bologna Reform in Ukraine: Learning Europeanisation in the post-soviet context*. Emerald Publishing Limited.

Kushnir, I. (2021b). The role of the European Education Area in European Union integration in times of crises. *European Review*, *30*(3), 301–321. https://doi.org/10.1017/S1062798721000016

Kushnir, I. (2023). 'It is more than just education. It's also a peace policy': (Re)imagining the mission of the European Higher Education Area in the context of the Russian invasion of Ukraine. *European Educational Research Journal*. https://doi.org/10.1177/14749041231200927

Kushnir, I., & Brooks, R. (2022). UK membership(s) in the European Higher Education Area post-2020: A 'Europeanisation' agenda. *European Educational Research Journal*, *22*(5), 718–740. https://doi.org/10.1177/14749041221083073

Kushnir, I., & Yazgan, N. (2024). *Shifting geopolitics of the European higher education space*. European Journal of Higher Education.

Mendick, H., & Peters, A. K. (2022). How post-Bologna policies construct the purposes of higher education and students' transitions into Masters programmes. *European Educational Research Journal*, *22*(2). https://doi.org/10.1177/14749041221076633

Pires Pereira, Í.S., Fernandes, E. L., Braga, A. C., & Flores, M. A. (2021). Initial teacher education after the Bologna Process. Possibilities and challenges for a renewed scholarship of teaching and learning. *European Journal of Teacher Education*, *46*(2), 1–29. https://doi.org/10.1080/02619768.2020.1867977

Polyakova, A. (2016). The great European unravelling? *World Policy Journal*, *33*(4), 68–72. https://doi.org/10.1215/07402775-3813051

Robertson, S., de Azevedo, M., & Dale, R. (2016). Higher education, the EU and the cultural political economy of regionalism. In S. L. Robertson, K. Olds, R. Dale, & Q. A. Dang (Eds.), *Global regionalisms and higher education* (pp. 24–28). Edward Elgar Publishing.

Robertson, S. L., Olds, K., & Dale, R. (2022). From the EHEA to the EEA: Renewed state-making ambitions in the regional governance of education in Europe. In M. Klemenčič (Ed.), *From actors to reforms in European higher education: A Festschrift for Pavel Zgaga* (pp. 65–76). Springer International Publishing.

Stake, R. E. (1994). Case studies. In N. K. Denzin & Y. S. Lincoln (Eds.), *Handbook of qualitative research*. Sage Publication.

Toens, K. (2009). The Bologna Process in German educational federalism: State strategies, policy fragmentation and interest mediation. *German Politics*, *18*(2), 246–264. https://doi.org/10.1080/09644000902870875

Veiga, A. (2023). Unthinking the European Higher Education Area: Differentiated integration and Bologna's different configurations. In C. Dienel (Ed.), *Globalizing higher education and strengthening the European spirit* (pp. 93–110). Routledge.

Veiga, A., Magalhaes, A., & Amaral, A. (2015). Differentiated integration and the Bologna Process. *Journal of Contemporary European Research, 11*(1), 84–102. https://doi.org/10.30950/jcer.v11i1.624

Zahavi, H., & Friedman, Y. (2019). The Bologna Process: An international higher education regime. *European Journal of Higher Education, 9*(1), 23–39. https://doi.org/10.1080/21568235.2018.1561314

Chapter 2

The Neo-Institutionalist Approach

Authored by Iryna Kushnir and Nuve Yazgan

Abstract

This chapter provides a detailed explanation of neo-institutionalism, which serves as an underlying theoretical framework for the analysis in this book. This explanation is constructed through a review of relevant theoretical literature as well as empirical studies that have applied neo-institutionalism. This chapter also explains how the analysis in this book attempts to turn the limitations of the theory into opportunities for analysis and what potential this theory has, particularly for the analysis of the research findings which are presented in this book.

Keywords: Neo-institutionalism; new institutionalism; institutionalism; historical neo-institutionalism; rational choice neo-institutionalism; sociological neo-institutionalism; discursive neo-institutionalism

2.1 Introduction

In addition to neo-institutionalism (NI) (Delreux, 2024), there have, of course, been other theories applied to the analysis of the European project, such as institutionalism and intergovernmentalism (Jones, 2018), new intergovernmentalism (Falkner, 2016), liberal intergovernmentalism (Borzel & Risse, 2018), federalism (Liargovas & Papageorgiou, 2024), functionalism, neofunctionalism (Borzel & Risse, 2018) and postfunctionalism (Schmidt, 2024), transactionalism and new supranationalism (Falkner, 2016). Consensus is missing as to which theory is the most suitable for the analysis of the European project. For instance, Falkner (2016) maintains that new intergovernmentalism may be emerging as a dominant theory in European Studies, but Borzel and Risse (2018) argue that neofunctionalism, postfunctionalism and liberal intergovernmentalism are the key theories. However, many of these approaches are tightly interrelated and some share nearly identical features, such as neo-institutionalism and postfunctionalism (Schmidt, 2024).

The analysis in this book of the role of European cooperation in higher education, represented by the initiatives of the European Higher Education Area (EHEA), in understanding the evolving mission of the European project in the early 2020s is informed by NI, given the focus of this approach on (formal) institutions (the EHEA in this case) that 'operate and develop mobilities, collaborations, interdependencies and interrelationships between central and state institutions, in shaping the right climate for transactions and policy development' (Liargovas & Papageorgiou, 2024, p. 13).

This chapter serves as a guide to NI as an underlying theoretical frame for this book. This chapter reviews relevant theoretical literature as well as examples of empirical studies that have been informed by NI in order to detail the essence of this theoretical approach, its development, current strands, limitations and potential. The chapter also explains how the analysis in this book attempts to turn the limitations of the theory into opportunities for analysis and what potential the theory has got particularly for the analysis of the research findings which are presented in this book.

2.2 Locating Institutionalist Approaches

Institutionalism is an umbrella term used in political science and related fields to analyse organisational behaviour by examining how institutions interact with one another and with the society (Ansell, 2021). We can refer to institutionalist scholarship as *old institutionalism* due to the emergence of the *'new' institutionalist theory* in the second half of the 20th century. Old institutionalism emerged in the early 20th century and was influential in the development of the American political science. The roots of 'old' institutionalism are based on the establishment of the political science discipline in the late 19th century and the works of a few classical sociologists, such as Max Weber and Emile Durkheim (Peters, 2019).

Overall, institutionalist approaches (including both their old and new versions) can be located within the broader context of political science when we look at public policy theories. Public policy theories, such as the Advocacy Coalition Framework, the Multiple Streams Framework, the Network Approach and the Punctuated Equilibrium Theory (Sabatier & Weible, 2014), focus on the processes through which policies are developed, implemented, and evaluated. These theories emphasise the importance of policy actors, such as interest groups, political parties, and bureaucracies, in shaping policy outcomes. These public policy theories also consider the role of policy feedback and evaluation in shaping future policy decisions. Old and new institutionalism provides an overall understanding of the political environment for policy processes with the focus on institutions rather than looking specifically at how policies are developed and implemented. For instance, the Advocacy Coalition Framework emphasises the role of interest groups and coalitions in shaping policy outcomes (Sabatier & Jenkins-Smith, 1993), while the Multiple Streams Framework suggests that policies are the result of the convergence of policy problems, policy solutions and political opportunities (Zahariadis, 2007). Overall, institutionalist approaches and the public policy theories mentioned above offer complementary perspectives on the study of politics and provide important insights into the workings of government and policymaking processes.

2.3 Old Institutionalism and New Institutionalism

Scholarship on both the old and new institutionalist approaches is complex. Consensus is missing as to what an institution is, what exactly new/neo institutionalism means and how different it is from the old version of institutionalism (Cairney, 2019). Nevertheless, the below is an attempt to capture and summarise key principles of the old and new versions of institutionalist approaches and, in particular, highlight key principles on which NI rests, as this is essential for the analysis later in this book.

Old institutionalism emphasised the role of law in governing, the role of structures, holism and historicism (Peters, 2019). Apart from these, old institutionalism had a strong normative objective with a concern for 'good governance' (Peters, 2019, p. 13); it also focused on assessing formal institutions and how they are responsible to the government (Rhodes, 1995). Old institutionalists were particularly interested in the role of institutions in maintaining political stability and preserving democratic norms. Overall, old institutionalism was not about theory building as it was rather a descriptive approach instead of a theory development platform (Shepsle, 1989).

NI, because it emerged as a response to the shortcomings of the earlier institutionalist approach, emphasises different aspects of institutional behaviour and development. NI is a theoretical stance that enables the analysis of organisational behaviour by focusing on how organisations, both formal and informal, interact among one another and with a wider society, and more importantly, how organisations change under the influence of wider processes – in other words, contextual factors that influence these organisations and are, in turn, influenced by them (Peters, 2019).

The behavioural and rational choice movements which emerged in the 1950s in political science can be considered as the background of the NI approach. Those movements focused on the development of the NI theory and an anti-normative bias (Peters, 2019). NI is opposed to the normative character of the old institutionalist approach, concerned with promoting 'good governance' (Peters, 2019, p. 13). According to Peters (2019), the NI emphasises methodology and theoretical advancement.

The term *NI* was introduced by Marc R. Tool in his doctoral thesis in 1953 (Tool, 1953). NI was developing from Clarence E. Ayres' integration of Veblen's evolutionary theory of institutions with John Dewey's theory of instrumental valuation (Bush, 2009). Gruchy's (1984) work offered another key development for NI as it provided a holistic approach to institutional economics. Comparatively, Gruchy's take on NI was more encompassing than Tool's explanation

(Almeida & De Silva, 2020). However, these perspectives on NI developed with no clear research programme and no methodology (Almeida & De Silva, 2020). Peters (2019, p. 2) states that 'new institutionalism is not a single animal but rather a genus with number of specific species within it'. Whereas all (neo)-institutionalists agree that institutions are important, there is no consensus on how and why they matter (Cairney, 2019).

The above suggests that there are differences between the old and new institutionalist approaches. Unlike old institutionalism, which focused on formal institutions such as legislatures, courts, and executives (Judge, 2008), NI recognises both formal and informal rules. The NI approach gained a lot of popularity in the late 1980s, and seminal studies, including foundational texts by DiMaggio and Powell (1983), Hall and Taylor (1996) and Shepsle (1989), were developed during this period. Given that old institutionalism focused only on a limited range of formal institutions suggests that the view of institutions in old institutionalism was quite limited. Therefore, one major difference of NI is its definition of institutions which comprises both formal and informal rules and ways of governing (Cairney, 2019; Hadler, 2015). NI deals with a variety of state and societal institutions that shape relations of political actors with other power groups by defining their interests (Steinmo et al., 1992). For example, the analysis of institutions in NI may include 'the rules of electoral competition, the structure of party systems, the relations among various branches of government, and the structure and organization of economic actors like trade unions' (Steinmo et al., 1992, p. 2). NI's view of institutions is rather flexible and inclusive compared to old institutionalism's rigid definitions.

How and why institutions change is the main question that is scrutinised by NI. NI has made the case for the characteristics of institutional change that will be discussed below. Overall, NI has focused more on the rules than organisations themselves, informality of their functioning rather than formality, as well as a dynamic view of institutional development (Lowndes, 2010), demonstrating the necessity of conceptualising institutions as independent variables (Rinas, 2021).

Such an interconnected and dynamic nature of modern organisations and their proneness to influences is the very reason for the recent preference for the term 'organisations' in the scholarship on NI, rather than 'institutions' which was a more common term in the earlier version of this theoretical approach – institutionalism (Peters, 2019). Nevertheless, in this book, the terms *institutions*, *organisations*, *stakeholders* and *actors* are used interchangeably to reflect the rhetoric of all institutionalist approaches as well as the language used in the empirical data sourced for the analysis (see the next chapters).

NI has provided theory development through empirical studies on its four strands which are discussed below. The historical, sociological, rational-choice strands and – recently – the discursive strand of NI have contributed to the advancement of this theory and related literature by employing a variety of methodologies. These four strands have also been useful in shaping the foci of analyses in contrast to old institutionalism which lacked causal mechanisms to explain the complexity of policy and political processes.

2.4 Four Strands of New Institutionalism

There are four key interconnected strands of NI: historical, sociological, rational choice (Peters, 2019) and discursive NI (Schmidt, 2014). All these four strands consider institutions as the main variables in analysing political phenomena.

2.4.1 The Historical Strand

The historical strand of NI focuses on the importance of the historical context and the path-dependent nature of institutional development, in which past decisions and events shape current institutional structures and practices. This strand of NI emerged as a reaction to behaviouralism (Lecours, 2005). The behaviouralist movement in political science became popular in the 1950s and 1960s, focusing on examining only observable behaviour of political actors (Easton, 1965). Behaviouralism advocates that the political behaviour of individuals should be studied instead of that of organisations or organisational units.

The historical strand of NI assumes that institutional development follows a particular path (Mahoney, 2000; Pierson & Skocpol, 2002). Path dependency means that the timing of any developmental incidents crucially affects their consequences. This means that path dependence creates a continuous institutional path in organisational development due to the logic of increasing returns (Mahoney, 2000). The historical strand rejects the idea that similar forces operating in similar ways will produce the same outcomes. Therefore, this strand of NI underlines the importance of 'critical junctures' which can be defined as 'brief phases of institutional flux… during which more dramatic change is possible' (Capoccia & Kelemen, 2007, p. 341). As Pierson (2000, p. 75) argues, 'what makes a particular juncture critical is that it triggers a process of positive feedback'. Institutional change happens through external shocks and institutional tensions (Lecours, 2005). Institutional structures make institutions resistant to evolution and change which can take many decades. By contrast to rational-choice NI discussed below, historical NI sees institutions as the processes of change with no defined end points (Farrell, 2018). Path dependency is an important factor to consider when analysing the role of higher education in the European project. Following the logic of the historical strand of NI, the situation post-2020, which is the focus of this book, is rooted in the pre-2020 developments.

2.4.2 The Sociological Strand

The sociological strand of NI focuses on social elements of institutions that include 'symbol systems, cognitive scripts and moral templates that provide the frames of meaning guiding human behaviour' (Hall & Taylor, 1996, p. 947). For sociological NI, institutions are organising myths (Farrell, 2018). Originating from the works of Weber and Durkheim, sociological NI has placed its prime focus on explaining interaction between organisations and individuals. Individuals play an important role in shaping organisational responses (Ansell, 2021; Hall, 2019). Sociological NI assumes that organisations follow social expectations in their organisational environments, which consist of individuals that define the organisational field (DiMaggio & Powell, 1983).

The emphasis of the sociological strand on the interaction between organisations and individuals is not the prime focus in this study, but we recognise the paramount role of individuals in shaping organisational responses from the Bologna stakeholders in each of the four countries that founded the EHEA. Hence, the individuals that represent these EHEA stakeholders are, *sine quaestione*, valuable sources of information about how these organisations form their responses.

2.4.3 The Rational-Choice Strand

The rational-choice strand of NI is based on 'methodological individualism' and explains political outcomes as aggregated decisions of political players (i.e. individuals and/or organisations or their units) involved. This strand mainly borrows its ideas from economics with a close look on the origins of US congressional institutions as theorised by American scholars (Bell, 2002). According to Rakner (1996), political organisations can include high-level policymakers such as government ministers, elected officials and others, from bureaucrats to low level policy actors such as local governments, think thanks, labour unions. Political actors can be a diverse group of individuals and organisational units who have a role in shaping policy and politics.

The rational-choice strand of NI assumes that actors are rational and their behaviour 'takes the form of choices based on either intelligent calculation or internalised rules that reflect optimal adaptation to experience' (Shepsle, 1989, p. 1340). Policymakers are expected to confirm with the rules and norms of an institution following a 'logic of appropriateness' (March & Olsen, 2006, p. 7). It is often individuals within organisations, whose preferences shape actions within the institutional context (Dowding & King, 1995). Also, their preferences are determined by the institutional environment (Bell, 2002). From the perspective of the rational-choice NI, institutions can be defined as structures or equilibria (Farrell, 2018). Structures are 'forces which conduct actors to select one equilibrium or another' and equilibria are 'sets of strategies from which no actor has any incentive to defect if no other actor defects' (Farrell, 2018, p. 27). Policymakers shape organisations based on rational objectives and they influence shaping institutional environments based of these objectives (Bell, 2002).

One example on these can be on the processes of European integration. Graziano and Vink (2017, p. 40) eloquently explicated that the rational choice strand highlights 'the increasing political opportunities provided by European integration' and resulting 'strategic organizational adaptation displayed by interest groups... when domestic political actors "rationally" use European resources in order to support predefined preferences'. This example shows how the rational calculations of various policymakers can shape political institutions that represent the European project, relying on higher education stakeholders in shaping its mission.

2.4.4 The Discursive Strand

The discursive strand of NI emphasises the role of discourse in institutional change (Carstensen & Schmidt, 2015; Schmidt, 2008, 2010, 2011, 2014; Widmaier, 2015). This strand suggests that it is specifically discursive processes that are beneficial to unravel 'why some ideas become the policies, programs, and philosophies that dominate political reality while others do not' (Schmidt, 2008, p. 309). These considerations have informed methodological choices for the project reported in this book as the review of official communications of the Bologna stakeholders was accompanied by interviews with the representations from key Bologna stakeholders to find out more information about policy decisions spelled out in the official communications.

The discursive strand of NI advocates the idea that discourse can be coordinative and communicative (Schmidt, 2008). Coordinative discourse is associated with the discourse of broader policy actors who engage with the development of policy ideas, such as in the case of government representatives who can align their actions and coordinate their efforts to achieve mutually beneficial outcomes (Schmidt, 2010). In contrast, communicative discourse relates to the discourse promoted by a variety of political actors who deal with 'formulation, modification and elaboration of ideas to persuade the public' (Schmidt, 2011, p. 171). Coordinative discourse happens between different policy actors, for instance, between the government and interest groups, while communicative discourse takes place between the political actors and the public (Schmidt, 2008).

Political actors use coordinative discourse to establish shared meanings and understandings that guide their actions and interactions with others. This can involve the use of shared terminology, symbols and narratives that create a sense of common purpose and identity among actors. Communicative discourse is directed to the public on the necessity of selected policies or actions of the political actors (Schmidt, 2008). Ideas that shape discourse come in various forms: frames, narratives, stories, memories (Schmidt, 2014). Institutional rules and norms are reflected in the ideas developed in a policy discourse that can be more flexible than organisational structures themselves (Cairney, 2015). Similarly, to the other three strands of NI that focus on organisational dynamics, the discursive strand is also focused on organisational change and can, arguably, be viewed sometimes as a contextual background of the organisational processes studied by other strands of NI, as discourse production is always part of what organisations do.

2.5 The Limitations of New Institutionalism

There is no perfect theory for studying organisational processes and political phenomena; otherwise, we would have singled it out a long time ago, disregarding all other approaches to such an analysis. Like any other theoretical direction, NI has been subject to criticism. It is important to review this criticism to develop a better understanding of NI and its applicability to the analysis of countries' memberships in the EHEA and their link to the evolving European project. While some criticism of NI is about its core assumptions, other critical points are more about the application of NI.

First, as discussed above, there is a huge diversity in NI which can be attributed to the new institutionalists themselves, particularly those setting off on a journey to make sense of NI (Lecours, 2005). Apart from different assumptions about what institutions are, why they matter and how to explain change and continuity in an institutional setting, there is no consensus on how to identify which branch of NI is most suited for a particular study. According to Peters (2019), on the one hand, different strands of NI are associated with quite different aims for analysis that may question the potential of the NI theory to provide holistic answers to any policy change. On the other hand, scholarly efforts to maintain the boundaries of the four strands may fall short on not recognising unavoidable overlaps among the aims of the four strands. For this reason, the analysis that follows in this book is informed by all four strands, although the rational-choice strand will dominate the analysis, given the emphasis on *strategic* decisions of the Bologna stakeholders.

The second point of criticism of NI mainly relates to its rational-choice strand's assumption that policy actors are rational beings. The so-called bounded rationality idea, developed by Simon (1990), explains this. Simon (1990) argues that actors have cognitive and resources-related limitations which prevent them from considering and calculating all possible alternatives. Therefore, bounded rationality limits actors in their effort to maximise utility within the institutional environment. This also relates to the rational-choice NI's assumption that external factors can cause ambiguous and multifaceted preferences of policy actors (Hall & Taylor, 1996). This criticism may also be relevant to other strands of NI. However, sourcing insights from all four strands should limit the drawbacks explained in this second point of criticism of NI.

Third, the growth of the feminist voice in NI has criticised the gender blindness of the institutionalist literature arguing for the necessity of bringing in a social justice lens, such as the gender lens, into the field of organisational analysis (Kenny, 2007; Mackay et al., 2010; Mackay & Waylen, 2009). These ideas later triggered the application of NI in the analysis of such issues as the impact of institutions on women's political participation (Huang, 2018) and gender mainstreaming in the EU (Minto & Mergaert, 2018).

The last major point of criticism of NI is related to its application, unlike the previous three points listed above which were more about fundamental ideas of NI. NI has been vigorously challenged in recent years by the scholars of organisation studies. Some organisation studies scholars argued that the definition of institutions ended up being blurred (Alvesson & Spicer, 2019; David & Bitektine, 2009) as 'institutions have become everything' (Alvesson & Spicer, 2019, p. 205). While we see the point that the nature of institutions has become all-encompassing, the study reported in this book focuses on a concrete list of organisations that are recognised on the EHEA website as Bologna stakeholders for each country.

Aside from this, some scholars criticise NI for not accounting for all the processes of institutionalisation and not considering the role of individuals within these institutionalisation processes (Hasselbladh & Kallinikos, 2000). Clearly, this criticism cannot relate to the sociological strand of NI, as it is explained earlier that its focus is predominantly on the role of individuals in organisations, which is something considered in the methodology of the study that is reported in this book.

2.6 The Potential of New Institutionalism

The three points of criticism of NI explicated above are important to be aware of, given that NI informs the study discussed in this book. However, as mentioned before, the limitations of NI should not be viewed as drawbacks of the theory per se, given that there is no theory in political science that has not faced criticism. Rather, these limitations should be used as additional points of analysis of the matter in focus.

In terms of NI's applicability, it has served as a useful theoretical lens for different areas of scholarship, including political science, economics, sociology and organisational studies. It has produced rich literature on institutions, their impact and how they shape individuals. Clearly, this evident flexible applicability of NI in different areas of research is a great advantage of this theory. Various scholars discussed the applicability of the NI theory (Bell, 2002; Cairney, 2015; Peters, 2019). For example, NI has been applied to the study of policy networks which include diverse actors and their interactions in a given policy environment (Bell, 2002). Therefore, institutional elements can be crucial for examining policy networks. Another example of NI's flexible applicability is its adoption in entrepreneurship literature (Zhai & Su, 2019). Scholars have focused on things like institutional drivers of entrepreneurship (Estrin & Mickiewicz, 2011) and the process of institutional entrepreneurship (Ansari & Phillips, 2011). One more example is from the literature on the organisational theory studies. Scholars have adopted the NI lens to examine, for instance, corporate social responsibility (Paynter et al., 2018) and corporative advantage (Bresser & Millonig, 2003).

This book applies NI to the analysis of countries' membership in the EHEA and its wider strategic importance for the development of the European project. The book is focused on a very particular range of institutions, identified through their relationship to the Bologna Process (BP). As explained elsewhere in the book, key organisations related to the implementation of the BP in the four founding countries of the EHEA, pre-identified on its official website (EHEA, 2023). They matter due to them shaping the nature of the memberships of the signatory countries in the EHEA and their strategic importance.

The emphasis on this strategic importance is aligned closely with the principles of the rational-choice strand of NI, given its preoccupation with rationalising actors' choices as in the case here – the strategising behind continuing memberships. This is not to disregard the bounded nature of policy actors' rationality (Simon, 1990) but rather to uncover what is possible in the rational decisions that have been made by relevant policy actors. While the rational-choice strand of NI dominates the analysis that follows in this book, the analysis does not overlook the overlaps among the four strands of NI. Indeed, the analysis that follows recognises the importance of the historical strand in presenting and relying on important contextual information about the development of Europe (see the next chapter) which is key for understanding how Europeanisation politics features in the strategies of Italy, France, Germany and the United Kingdom in continuing their roles in the EHEA. The methodology for data collection for this book (e.g. interviews with representatives of key stakeholders) is, in part, informed by sociological NI which emphasises the role that individuals play in shaping organisational responses (Peters, 2019). Finally, the data gathered from the interviews and stakeholders' official communications cannot overlook the fact that the discourse created by these organisations and individuals that represent them shapes the essence of our understanding of the processes that are analysed. This is precisely what the discursive strand of NI is preoccupied with. Finally, given the reliance of the book on the rational-choice strand predominantly and the recent growth of the criticism of this strand advocating the idea that the issues of social justice should feature more in NI analyses, the book addresses this in, for instance, analysing the response of the Bologna stakeholders in the founding countries of the EHEA to the invasion of Ukraine.

Evidently, despite the criticism that NI has faced, it remains a popular and influential framework for understanding the workings not only of organisations per se but also of the wider society. This is due to the inextricable link between the two domains.

2.7 Conclusion

This chapter has offered an extensive explanation of the NI theory which informs the analysis in this book, focused on the role of European cooperation in higher education, represented by the EHEA initiatives, in understanding the evolving mission of the European project in the early 2020s.

This explanation of NI was constructed through a review of relevant theoretical literature as well as empirical studies that have applied NI. This chapter has also explained how the analysis in this book attempts to turn the recognised limitations of the theory into opportunities for analysis and what potential the theory has got particularly for the analysis of the research project which is presented in this book.

References

Almeida, F., & De Silva, V. C. (2020). Allan Gruchy's view of institutionalism and the foundation and early years of the association for evolutionary economics. *EconomiA*, *21*(3), 394–406. https://doi.org/10.1016/j.econ.2020.09.001

Alvesson, M., & Spicer, A. (2019). Neo-institutional theory and organization studies: A mid-life crisis? *Organization Studies*, *40*(2), 199–218. https://doi.org/10.1177/0170840618772610

Ansari, S. S., & Phillips, N. (2011). Text me! New consumer practices and change in organizational fields. *Organization Science*, *22*(6), 1579–1599. https://doi.org/10.1287/orsc.1100.0595

Ansell, C. (2021). Institutionalism. In M. Riddervold, J. Trondal, & A. Newsome (Eds.), *The Palgrave handbook of EU crises* (pp. 135–152). Palgrave Macmillan. https://doi.org/10.1007/978-3-030-51791-5

Bell, S. (2002). Institutionalism. In J. Summers, D. Woodward, & A. Parkin (Eds.), *Government, politics, power and policy in Australia* (pp. 363–380). Pearson Education Australia.

Borzel, T., & Risse, T. (2018). From the euro to the Schengen crises: European integration theories, politicization, and identity politics. *Journal of European Public Policy*, *25*(1), 83–108. https://doi.org/10.1080/13501763.2017.1310281

Bresser, R. K., & Millonig, K. (2003). Institutional capital: Competitive advantage in light of the new institutionalism in organization theory. *Schmalenbach Business Review*, *55*, 220–241. https://EconPapers.repec.org/RePEc:sbr:abstra:v:55:y:2003:i:3:p:220-241

Bush, P. D. (2009). The neoinstitutionalist theory of value: Remarks upon receipt of the Veblen-Commons Award. *Journal of Economic Issues*, *43*(2), 293–307. https://doi.org/10.2753/JEI0021-3624430202

Cairney, P. (2015). How can policy theory have an impact on policymaking? The role of theory-led academic–practitioner discussions. *Teaching Public Administration*, *33*(1), 22–39.

Cairney, P. (2019). *Understanding public policy: Theories and issues*. Bloomsbury Publishing. ISBN 9781137545183.

Capoccia, G., & Kelemen, R. D. (2007). The study of critical junctures: Theory, narrative, and counterfactuals in historical institutionalism. *World Politics*, *59*(3), 341–369. https://doi.org/10.1017/S0043887100020852

Carstensen, M. B., & Schmidt, V. A. (2015). Power through, over and in ideas: Conceptualizing ideational power in discursive institutionalism. *Journal of European Public Policy*, *23*(3), 1–20. https://doi.org/10.1080/13501763.2015.1115534

David, R., & Bitektine, A. (2009). De deinstitutionalization of institutional theory? In D. Buchanan & A. Bryman (Eds.), *The Sage handbook of organizational research methods*. SAGE Publications. ISBN 10 1446200647.

Delreux, T. (2024). New institutionalism. In *Handbook on European Union public administration* (pp. 22–33). Edward Elgar Publishing.

DiMaggio, P. J., & Powell, W. W. (1983). The iron cage revisited: Institutional isomorphism and collective rationality in organizational fields. *American Sociological Review*, *48*(2), 147–160. https://doi.org/10.2307/2095101

Dowding, K. M., & King, D. S. (1995). *Preferences, institutions, and rational choice*. Oxford University Press. ISBN 9780198278955.

Easton, D. (1965). *A framework for political analysis*. Prentice Hall. https://doi.org/10.1177/000271626536000117

EHEA. (2023). Official website. https://ehea.info/. Accessed on April 19, 2023.

Estrin, S., & Mickiewicz, T. (2011). Institutions and female entrepreneurship. *Small Business Economics*, *37*(4), 397–415. http://www.jstor.org/stable/41486142

Falkner, G. (2016). The EU's current crisis and its policy effects: Research design and comparative findings. *Journal of European Integration*, *38*(3), 219–235. https://doi.org/10.1080/07036337.2016.1140154

Farrell, H. (2018). The shared challenges of institutional theories: Rational choice, historical institutionalism, and sociological institutionalism. *Knowledge and Institutions*, 23–44. https://doi.org/10.1007/978-3-319-75328-7_2

Graziano, P., & Vink, M. (2017). Europeanization: Concept, theory, and methods. In S. Bulmer & C. Lequesne (Eds.), *The member states of the European Union* (pp. 31–54). Oxford University Press. https://doi.org/10.1093/hepl/9780199544837.003.0002

Gruchy, A. G. (1984). Neo institutionalism, neo-Marxism, and neo-Keynesianism: An evaluation. *Journal of Economic Issues, 18*(2), 547–556.

Hadler, M. (2015). Institutionalism and neo-institutionalism: History of the concepts. In J. Wright (Ed.), *International encyclopedia of the social and behavioral sciences* (pp. 186–189). Elsevier. ISBN 9780080970875.

Hall, C. (2019). *Social work as narrative: Storytelling and persuasion in professional texts*. Routledge.

Hall, P. A., & Taylor, R. C. (1996). Political Science and the three new institutionalisms. *Political Studies, 44*(5), 936–957. https://doi.org/10.1111/j.1467-9248.1996.tb00343.x

Hasselbladh, H., & Kallinikos, J. (2000). The project of rationalization: A critique and reappraisal of neo-institutionalism in organization studies. *Organization Studies, 21*(4), 697–720. https://doi.org/10.1177/0170840600214002

Huang, C. (2018). Why low political participation of rural women in China: An interpretation from neo-institutionalism perspective. *Open Journal of Political Science, 8*(03), 250. https://doi.org/10.4236/ojps.2018.83018

Jones, E. (2018). Towards a theory of disintegration. *Journal of European Public Policy, 25*(3), 440–451. https://doi.org/10.1080/13501763.2017.1411381

Judge, D. (2008). *Institutional theory and legislatures*. Manchester University Press.

Kenny, M. (2007). Gender, institutions and power: A critical review. *Politics, 27*(2), 91–100. https://doi.org/10.1111/j.1467-9256.2007.00284.x

Lecours, A. (Ed.). (2005). *New institutionalism: Theory and analysis* (Vol. 23). University of Toronto Press. https://doi.org/10.3138/9781442677630

Liargovas, P., & Papageorgiou, C. (2024). Theoretical perspectives on European integration and its evolutionary trajectory. In *The European integration, Vol. 2: Institutions and policies* (pp. 11–55). Springer Nature Switzerland.

Lowndes, V. (2010). The institutional approach. In D. March & G. Stroker (Eds.), *Theory and methods in political science* (pp. 60–79). Palgrave. ISBN 9781137603517.

Mackay, F., Kenny, M., & Chappell, L. (2010). New institutionalism through a gender lens: Towards a feminist institutionalism? *International Political Science Review, 31*(5), 573–588. https://doi.org/10.1177/0192512110388788

Mackay, F., & Waylen, G. (2009). Critical perspectives on feminist institutionalism. *Politics and Gender, 5*(2), 237–280. https://doi.org/10.1017/S1743923X09000178

Mahoney, J. (2000). Path dependence in historical sociology. *Theory and Society, 29*(4), 507–548. https://www.jstor.org/stable/3108585

March, J. G., & Olsen, J. P. (2006). Elaborating the new institutionalism. In A. W. Rhodes, S. A. Binder, & B. A. Rockman (Eds.), *The Oxford handbook of political institutions* (pp. 3–22). Oxford University Press. https://doi.org/10.1093/oxfordhb/9780199548460.003.0001

Minto, R., & Mergaert, L. (2018). Gender mainstreaming and evaluation in the EU: Comparative perspectives from feminist institutionalism. *International Feminist Journal of Politics, 20*(2), 204–220. https://doi.org/10.1080/14616742.2018.1440181

Paynter, M., Halabi, A. K., & Lawton, A. (2018). The neo-institutionalism influences on corporate social responsibility reporting development in Australia: A three company study. In D. Crowther, S. Seifi, & A. Moyeen (Eds.), *The goals of sustainable development: Responsibility and governance* (pp. 193–214). Springer. https://doi.org/10.1007/978-981-10-5047-3

Peters, B. (2019). *Institutional theory in political science: The new institutionalism*. Edward Elgar Publishing. ISBN 9781786437921.

Pierson, P. (2000). Increasing returns, path dependence, and the study of politics. *American Political Science Review, 94*(02), 251–267. https://doi.org/10.2307/2586011

Pierson, P., & Skocpol, T. (2002). Historical institutionalism in contemporary political science. In I. Katznelson & H. Milner (Eds.), *Political science: The state of the discipline* (pp. 693–721). W. W. Norton. ISBN 0393978710.

Rakner, L. (1996) *Rational choice and the problem of institutions. A discussion of rational choice institutionalism and its application by Robert Bates*. Bergen. Chr. Michelsen Institute. CMI Working Paper WP, 1996(6).

Rhodes, R. A. W. (1995). The institutional approach. In D. Marsh & G. Stoker (Eds.), *Theory and methods in political science* (pp. 42–57). Macmillan.

Rinas, S. P. (2021). Institutionalism in the 21st century. In S. P. Rinas (Ed.), *From telecommunications liberalization to net neutrality rules: A longitudinal institutional analysis of EU communications policy* (pp. 15–71). Springer. ISBN 3658330139.

Sabatier, P. A., & Jenkins-Smith, H. C. (1993). *Policy change and learning: An advocacy coalition framework*. Westview. ISBN 0813316499.

Sabatier, P. A., & Weible, C. M. (2014). *Theories of the policy process*. Westview. https://doi.org/10.4324/9780429494284

Schmidt, V. A. (2008). Discursive institutionalism: The explanatory power of ideas and discourse. *Annual Review of Political Science, 11*, 303–326. https://doi.org/10.1146/annurev.polisci.11.060606.135342

Schmidt, V. A. (2010). Taking ideas and discourse seriously: Explaining change through discursive institutionalism as the fourth "new institutionalism". *European Political Science Review, 2*(1), 1–25. https://doi.org/10.1017/S175577390999021X

Schmidt, V. A. (2011). Reconciling ideas and institutions through discursive institutionalism. In D. Béland & R. H. Cox (Eds.), *Ideas and politics in social science research* (pp. 47–64). Oxford University Press. https://doi.org/10.1093/acprof:oso/9780199736430.001.0001

Schmidt, V. A. (2014). Speaking to the markets or to the people? A discursive institutionalist analysis of the EU's sovereign debt crisis. *The British Journal of Politics & International Relations, 16*(1), 188–209. https://doi.org/10.1111/1467-856X.12023

Schmidt, V. A. (2024). Theorising European integration: The four phases since Ernst Haas' original contribution. *Journal of European Public Policy*, 1–26.

Shepsle, K. A. (1989). Studying institutions: Some lessons from the rational choice approach. *Journal of Theoretical Politics, 1*(2), 131–147. https://doi.org/10.1177/0951692889001002002

Simon, H. A. (1990). Bounded rationality. In J. Eatwell, M. Milgate, & P. Newman (Eds.), *Utility and probability* (pp. 15–18). Palgrave Macmillan. https://doi.org/10.1007/978-1-349-20568-4

Steinmo, S., Thelen, K., & Longstreth, F. (1992). *Structuring politics: Historical institutionalism in comparative analysis*. Cambridge University Press. https://doi.org/10.1017/CBO9780511528125

Tool, M. R. (1953). *The philosophy of neo-institutionalism: Veblen, Dewey, and Ayres (Publication No. 9961200)*. Doctoral thesis, University of Colorado. ProQuest Dissertations and Theses Global.

Widmaier, W. (2015). The power of economic ideas–through, over and in–political time: The construction, conversion and crisis of the neoliberal order in the US and UK. *Journal of European Public Policy, 23*(3), 338–356. https://doi.org/10.1080/13501763.2015.1115890

Zahariadis, N. (2007). The multiple streams framework: Structure, limitations, prospects. In P. A. Sabatier (Ed.), *Theories of policy processes* (pp. 65–93). Westview. https://doi.org/10.4324/9780367274689

Zhai, Q., & Su, J. (2019). A perfect couple? Institutional theory and entrepreneurship research. *Chinese Management Studies*. https://doi.org/10.1108/CMS-07-2017-0194

Chapter 3

The European Project and European Higher Education

Authored by Iryna Kushnir

Abstract

This chapter maps the landscape of existing research on the European project and European higher education initiatives, focusing predominantly on the European Higher Education Area (EHEA). This literature explores key debates around the borders of the European project, analyses it as a space of meaning, the balance between unity and diversity within it, and its evolving mission, before delving into the relationship between the European project and the EHEA. This chapter also points out a few major gaps in that research.

Keywords: Europe; the European project; Europeanisation; European Higher Education Area; higher education; borders; space of meaning

3.1 Introduction

This chapter maps existing scholarship on the European project and European higher education initiatives, focusing primarily on the European Higher Education Area (EHEA). This chapter also considers some key theoretical ideas around the notion of Europe and its related terms, informed by the discussion of neo-institutionalism in the previous chapter. While the borders of the European Union (EU) have been a matter of political agreements, the European project has been developing as a space of meaning, that has increasingly been surpassing the borders of the EU, and aiming to unite Europe as a region the geography of which spans beyond EU's borders (Kushnir, 2016). As such, in this book, the terms *the European project* and *Europe* are used interchangeably.

3.2 The European Project

This section explores key debates around the borders of the European project, analyses it as a space of meaning and an ongoing balancing act between unity and diversity. Attention is also paid to its evolving mission. According to the logic of historical neo-institutionalism, explained in the previous chapter, this background information is a key historical context for scrutinising the relationship between the European project and the EHEA, available literature about which is reviewed at the end of this chapter.

3.2.1 Borders

Most of the perspectives on what Europe is concentrate on the idea of its borders. One example of this is the EU versus geographical Europe debate. The term *Europe* is very often used interchangeably with term *the European Union (EU)* (Bellier & Wilson, 2020; Novoa & Lawn, 2002; Papatsiba, 2009). There are even attempts in the earlier literature to emphasise the link between the two by capitalising the first two letters of the term 'EUrope' and its derivatives in order to make a connection to the spelling of the EU (Antonsich, 2008). This was the case even though geographically Europe extends further to the east from the EU border, covering some non-EU countries such as Moldova, Ukraine and even a small western part of Russia (Walters, 2009). However, more recent literature (e.g. Kočan, 2023, p. 15) points out flaws in such thinking and calls for distinguishing 'Europeanisation from EU-isation'.

3.2.2 A Space of Meaning

Scholars have been asking what the meaning of Europe is for a couple of decades (Datler et al., 2021; Meacham & de Warren, 2021; Olszewska, 2022) in the attempts to consolidate a uniform answer. This process suggests a degree of fluidity in the meaning of Europe as it is imagined. For this reason, Abélès (2020, p. 40) calls it a 'virtual Europe'. Similarly, Lawn and Grek (2012) recognise that the idea of borders is an example of conventional thinking about Europe because people are used to applying their conception of country boundaries to speculate about Europe. Nevertheless, apart from the focus on the issue of borders that define Europe, the authors argue that Europe is 'a space of meaning' rather than 'merely a place' (Lawn & Grek, 2012, p. 13).

This book is informed by Lawn and Grek's (2012) notion of Europe as 'a space of meaning' rather than 'merely a place' and acknowledges that both of these statements are two separate, but related, ways of viewing Europe. Lawn and Grek's (2012) thinking is extended here to suggest that Europe is, indeed, a space of meaning but it should not be seen as an idea separate from the view that it is still a place with borders. Rather, it should be viewed as including borders, which are also instrumental in shaping the meaning of Europe. Given the focus of the book on the EHEA and its link to Europe, in this book, Europe is seen as a space that expands European borders beyond the EU.

This book is also informed by the argument in my earlier paper (Kushnir, 2016, p. 665) that EHEA's 'Bologna Process contributes to defining Europe by changing its geopolitics through expanding its borders and promoting the idea of a common European identity within these borders.' This book only partly relies on this argument due to some significant changes that took place since the 2016 study. These changes include the subsiding of the focus in the EHEA on cultivating European identity and placing an emphasis on internationalisation as well as advocating social justice (Kushnir et al., 2024).

Lawn and Grek (2012) explain that the view of Europe as 'a space of meaning' builds on another concept – the 'imagined community'. This concept was introduced by Anderson in a broader context, not specifically Europe, with the intention of theorising nations and nationalism (Anderson, 1983, p. 15). Anderson stated that nations are imagined because while their members do not know one another, they all consider themselves to be part of one community. Nations are distinct because the ways in which they are imagined differ. As a result, nationalism is not about awakening a nation but about, in a way, inventing a nation. Lawn and Grek (2012) developed their notion of Europe as 'a space of meaning' based on these ideas, implying that the meaning of Europe depends on how and by whom it is imagined.

3.2.3 Unity and Diversity: A Balancing Act

It is also important to emphasise the challenges with regard to generating a homogenous meaning of European-ness within Europe. Derrida (1992) warns that the European identity-seeking process is about building commonality with respect for unavoidable differences. Derrida acknowledges that the respect for diversity is the only route for commonality to be facilitated in Europe. Trying to establish one centralised authority would only undermine the respect for diversity which is an integral part of European identity. A more recent study (Sassatelli, 2021, p. 195) has also highlighted the ideas of 'Europe's cosmopolitan identity' and 'unity in diversity'.

To unpack the essence of why unity and diversity in Europe that transcends the borders of the EU have to be balanced, let us review relevant issues that the EU itself has been facing. A lack of unity within the EU, as well as between the EU and its neighbours, has recently been noticeable with regard to a few challenges, such as in the disagreements about how to handle the post-2015 migrant crisis related to the arrival of refugees mainly from Syria. This 'migrant crisis' has uncovered a number of weaknesses in the EU, such as political divisions among the EU countries, the lack of the EU's preparedness to deal with such a crisis, a transparency deficit in the work of the EU institutions and questions around whether a common European identity existed at all (Taggart & Szczerbiak, 2018).

The biggest polemics concerned the Visegrad group (Poland, Czech Republic, Hungary and Slovakia) and the United Kingdom. What concerns the former regions, their 'drifting away' from the rest of the EU has been evident mainly because of Visegrad countries' reluctance to accept refugees (Nagy, 2017, p. 2).

Regarding the second region – the United Kingdom – its oppositional rhetoric to the EU was apparent long before the 'migrant crisis', such as in Fletcher's (2009, p. 71) analysis of the 'balancing of the United Kingdom's "Ins" and "Outs"' in the EU. This was a fertile ground for the migrant crisis to add fuel to the UK Leave Campaign as the 2016 Brexit Referendum was approaching (Sayer, 2017).

The 'migrant crisis' exposed another EU's weakness related to migration and refugee policy, specifically the gaps in the Common Asylum System (CAS), as well as with wider EU institutions. Despite some controversies over the CAS (Kugiel, 2016), the system had been working in the context of lower numbers before 2014 (Pastore & Henry, 2016). The inadequacy of CAS after 2015 had been part of a wider issue with the EU institutions. A perceived lack of transparency in the work of EU institutions predated the 'migrant crisis' (Follesdal & Hix, 2006). However, the sentiment was not as strong as afterwards.

The idea of a European identity started to be questioned more after the 'migrant crisis' as well (Clycq, 2021). In this context, it does not come as a surprise that Kushnir et al. (2020, p. 314) points out 'a new central place for migration policy in debates on EU integration.' Evidently, European politics started emphasising migration, but only in addition to education, the role of which has not decreased due to the work of the EHEA since 1998 and the European Education Area since 2017 (Kushnir, 2021). The work of the EHEA, in particular, which encompasses a lot more countries than the EU, points again to the idea of a growing reach of the European project explained earlier.

3.2.4 An Evolving Mission of the European Project

The mission of the European project has been an ongoing journey. A huge milestone in the consolidation of the peoples of Europe was the establishment of the EU. The main reason for its emergence was ensuring security on the continent and embarking on a peace-building mission. The fall of the Soviet Union and Yugoslavia back in 1991 contributed to this aspiration (Dedman, 2009). The Maastricht Treaty, signed in 1992 and ratified in 1993, established the EU initially with the membership of 12 countries. This consolidated the efforts to bring European people together. This also commenced a new phase in the evolution of the European project through a few important steps. They included launching the single market in 1993 and the European Economic Area in 1994 which, importantly, extended the single market beyond EU borders to include three members of the European Free Trade Association. Following this, border-free travel was enacted in 1995 by the Schengen Agreement. These developments were complemented and followed by working out how to reform EU institutions and facilitate European 'citizenship' in 1997 and launching the Euro in 1999. Several waves of EU enlargement followed to include neighbouring states in 1995, 2004, 2007 and 2013, ending up in the membership of 28 Member States (MSs) before Brexit (EU, 2024).

The EU was awarded the Nobel Peace Prize in 2012 for its achievements in the peace-building (Bebler, 2015) – the journey it embarked on after the WWII.

However, the time that these advancements took has gradually altered the sense of urgency and need for the post-war peace-building and security embodied in the development of the European project. Younger generations could not relate to those needs, and the bureaucratic procedures of the EU were not adding towards persuading them that the Union in such a form was a way forward (Polyakova, 2016). Moreover, new challenges such as dealing with forced migration came to be seen as a drawback of being in the Union (Taggart & Szczerbiak, 2018).

The search for the drivers of the European project continued. In this effort, European education emerged as such a uniting factor. Over a decade ago, Grek (2008, p. 208) argued that, '...education is slowly moving from the margins of European governance to the very centre of its policy making.' I have also highlighted (Kushnir, 2021) a similar tendency in how the European Education Area, as a series of initiatives for all levels of education in the EU MSs, has been used by EU decision-makers to facilitate the deepening of the relationships among the EU MSs in the context of various challenges they have been dealing with. Specifically, HE has played a key role in developing the European project through the facilitation of academic mobility, aiding the creation of the European single market and a European citizen (Robertson et al., 2016). This central role that education has started holding in the EU has been important but it did not turn out to be as uniting as the peace-building ideal that led to the establishment of the EU.

The main aim of the development of post-war institutions in Europe was to make another war on the European continent unthinkable and impossible. Nevertheless, those establishments started prioritising elite governance over popular participation. Resultingly, a Europe founded on education has, arguably, started appearing as a more truly people's Europe than what the post-war institutions have brought about for us. Education has then emerged as an instrument for defeating the lack of unity within the EU, and even more so, for developing deeper relationships between the EU MSs, as well as between them and their neighbouring countries.

3.3 Higher Education and the European Project

While the idea that HE has been instrumental to the development of the European project has been briefly mentioned, the below sheds more light on the relationship between European HE and the European project.

3.3.1 The Role of Higher Education in Europe Historically

The process of HE Europeanisation can be traced back to the period after World War II, when between the 1950s and the 1990s:

> ...the internationalization of study programmes, curricula, student mobility and research career paths was primarily oriented towards European partners and Europeanising processes. Key markers were the institutionalising of regular meetings between the

European education ministers, the eventual creation of the European University Institute in Florence in 1971, and the establishment of the EU's Erasmus mobility programme in 1987 to facilitate the movement of students and staff between universities of the member states. (Robertson et al., 2016, p. 28)

After this and the active development and enactment of joint academic mobility programmes (Scott, 2012), HE in Europe was viewed by the European Commission (EC) as a potential tool to help create a European single market and European citizen (Corbett, 2005). The issue of the 1991 Memorandum on Higher Education demonstrates that HE 'had already become part of the Community's broader agenda of economic and social coherence' (Huisman & Van Der Wende, 2004, p. 350). Furthermore, the aim of creating a common identity had gained momentum in light of the challenges of Americanisation and the collapse of the Soviet Union in 1991 (Grek, 2008). The necessity to reinforce the common identity of Europe led to signing the Treaty on European Union or the Maastricht Treaty in 1992 and enforcing it in 1993. Ironically, despite the fact that the Maastricht had been eagerly anticipated, enthusiasm decreased after it was signed (Grek, 2008). Grek (2008) suggests that this lack of support could only have been overcome once a unifying myth was found. The idea of common economic policies seemed not to have been sufficient enough to justify the European project. Instead, education in general, including HE, started emerging as a more influential factor of Europeanisation in the region (Grek, 2008).

The EC devised new tactics to develop a 'European dimension' in education by further consolidating the European HE space and looking for cooperation opportunities with other regions (Robertson et al., 2016). A range of collaborative programmes were established with non-EU states, for example: the América Latina – Formación Académica (ALFA) programme in Latin America; the Trans-European Mobility Programme for University Studies (TEMPUS) programme with the Western Balkans, Eastern Europe, Central Asia and some Mediterranean countries; and Asia-Link with Asia (Robertson, 2008). While these were significant developments, they tended to be based on cultural cooperation and idea exchange, and 'were not well coordinated with the emerging policy programme for education within Europe' (Robertson et al., 2016, p. 29). Mounting global pressures prompted the EU to seek a more coordinated strategy of building its economic competitiveness in different ways, including through HE by setting out to develop the EHEA.

It is also important to note that the EHEA has not been the only platform that allowed European cooperation in HE. EC Directorate General for Education and Culture has coordinated a number of initiatives that collectively came to be known as the Education and Training (ET) Work frameworks 2010/2020 which targeted mainly EU countries. Ionela and Camelia (2014, p. 330) state that both frameworks considered 'the whole spectrum of education and training systems from the perspective of lifelong learning, covering all levels and contexts (including non-formal and informal education)'. This proves that HE has been one of their priorities. Aside from this, there has been some overlap between EHEA's Bologna Process and ET 2010/2020. Ferreira and Mota (2019, p. 182) explain that 'The education and training programmes include the initiatives in the context of the inter-governmental platform for the Bologna Process'. While these ET frameworks did not represent a formalised EU education space, they paved way for it, which culminated in 2017 with the establishment of the European Education Area (EEA).

The EEA is an education policy harmonisation project specifically for the EU MSs (EC, 2020). Unlike the EHEA, the EEA is exclusively for the EU. The website of the EC (EC, 2020) details that the EEA is an EU project to enable 'all young people to benefit from the best education and training, and to find employment across Europe'. Moreover, unlike the EHEA, this is meant to be achieved through a range of initiatives across all levels and types of education: mutual recognition of diplomas, quality in early childhood education and care, language learning, key competencies for lifelong learning, digital education action plans, common values, European universities initiative and European student card initiative. The European universities initiatives have, arguably, gained the most momentum recently. However, similarly to ET 2010/2020, it has come to been associated with the EHEA as well (Moscovitz & Zahavi, 2020).

3.3.2 Learning to Build the EHEA

Scott (2012, p. 4) states that the 'action lines' that emerged in the EHEA were always negotiated in terms of a 'delicate balance between Europe-wide initiatives and the prerogatives of nation states.' The active development and enactment of joint academic mobility programmes, mentioned above, were underway even before the formal establishment of the EU through the Maastricht Treaty in 1993. For example, the *Erasmus* and *TEMPUS* programmes played a part in paving the way towards building the EHEA. Almost a decade of success of the Erasmus programme, which supported student mobility, contributed to forming the basis of the EHEA (Powell & Finger, 2013). The European Credit Transfer System (ECTS) was originally introduced in the Erasmus programme's framework to support student mobility through credit transfer (Weiss & Egea-Cortines, 2008). A decade later, it was taken up in the Bologna Process to be used as one of its action lines. A similar contribution was made by the TEMPUS programme, which was established in 1990 by the EC. TEMPUS aimed to promote and support the modernisation of HE in Western and Eastern Europe, Central Asia, and the Mediterranean region, mainly through university cooperation projects and individual mobility grants (Keeling, 2006).

Moreover, the diploma supplement was established by the Lisbon Recognition Convention in 1997 – a year before the first pre-Bologna international ministerial conference in 1998 – as a final transcript of grades and credits that students had to obtain after their studies. It became a Bologna action line from the onset of the Bologna Process with the aim to promote the recognition of degrees, as well as the mobility and employability of graduates (Vögtle, 2014).

These pre-Bologna developments created a foundation for the construction of the EHEA by establishing easily readable, comparable and recognisable degrees through a range of action lines. That said, the list of action lines presented by different scholars vary. This is not surprising – action lines are negotiated at biennial international ministerial conferences (EHEA, 2024) and are expanded and regrouped in international ministerial documents. As such, the Bologna Process, and therefore the EHEA, are often thought of as moving targets, as new elements are consistently added (Diogo, 2020; Teichler, 2012). Another perspective views the Bologna Process as a 'snowball' in the EHEA, as it attaches previous European HE developments to itself as it develops its action lines (Reichert, 2010; Scott, 2012; Vögtle & Martens, 2014). Such a combination of different HE aims in the EHEA prompted Veiga (2012, p. 389) to pose the following question: 'Could it be that the shift in policy discourse extended the scale of Bologna, thereby making it difficult to delineate clearly what in effect Bologna policy was(is) and what it was(is) not?'

The Bologna Process within the EHEA is also difficult to delineate because it crossed EU boarders to encompass the geographical Europe and some countries beyond it that are not commonly seen as European (e.g. Kazakhstan). This territorial expansion has called into question the meaning of *the European* in the European HE space. In this context, the term *European* does not mean *the EU* or its HE space. Nevertheless, the EHEA was the first and biggest formal all-encompassing HE space that involved EU countries and many of their neighbours, and transformed into an 'international higher education regime' (Zahavi & Friedman, 2019, p. 23).

3.4 Understanding the Gaps in Prior Research

There are three major interrelated gaps in the literature that sits on the intersection of the topics related to the European project and European HE. These gaps are related to the role of European HE represented by the EHEA initiatives in understanding the evolving mission of the European project in the post-2020 era, focusing on the early 2020s.

First and foremost, the four founders of the EHEA, particularly the interconnectedness of their EHEA membership agendas and their wider political agendas is a gap in existing research. This book relies on the insights of the representatives from key EHEA stakeholders in EHEA's four founding countries: Germany, France, Italy and the United Kingdom. There is a range of single-country or collective case studies that incorporated only some countries of my interest in the context of the EHEA. Most of the earlier studies focus on the implementation implications of the Bologna action lines and the process of relevant reforms (e.g. Antoniolli, 2006; Field, 2005; Guth, 2006; Malan, 2004). The foci of recent studies (Kushnir, 2023; Kushnir & Yazgan, 2023; Marquand & Scott, 2018) are more varied. For example, Marquand and Scott (2018) explain the difference of enthusiasm for the EHEA action lines in UK devolved governments. No other study places EHEA's founders jointly at the centre of attention. An exception is my recent article (Kushnir & Yazgan, 2023) which is informed by this same project and represents its extract. Part of the significance of this book lies in addressing this particular gap by exploring the interconnectedness of their EHEA membership agendas and their wider political agendas.

Second, prior scholarship on the link between the European project and the EHEA has not relied on neo-institutionalism in the analysis of Europeanisation politics in the context of EHEA memberships, which has scope to offer innovative perspectives, as illustrated by the upcoming chapters. Such an analysis from the neo-institutionalist lens is timely for theorising differentiated Europeanisation from the HE perspective and informing EHEA international level policy-making in the run-up to EHEA's new deadline of 2030 (EHEA, 2024). The first years after the 19 November, 2020, stocktaking ministerial meeting are crucial in shaping the directions of work of EHEA's signatories. Although the concept 'differentiated Europeanisation' stems from EU studies, it has also been applied to the analysis of the EHEA, the boundaries of which spread far beyond the EU. Two publications have applied it. Veiga et al. (2015) applied it, but only in the area of HE harmonisation and only in the context of Germany, Italy, Norway and Portugal. Even though Germany and Italy featured in that study, it did not answer the questions posed by the project reported in this book. This is because the scholars relied only on the analysis of country's Bologna reports prior to 2009, did not review the situation post-2020, did not offer an in-depth exploration of the perspectives of key HE actors on the EHEA membership and did not view it as a case of a wider Europeanisation agenda of the countries. Veiga's (2023) reflective article juxtaposes the discussion of differentiated integration in the EU and differences within the EHEA. However, while discussing Brexit, Veiga (2023) does not focus specifically on the timeframe after the 2020 EHEA's deadline and the war context in Ukraine. The scholar also does not focus on four EHEA's founders and does not inform their analysis by neo-institutionalism. It is essential to bridge the literature on the EHEA and wider Europeanisation particularly with regard to the countries that initiated the EHEA as a platform for Europeanisation to better understand the nature of Europeanisation.

Third and finally, the study reported in this book also addresses a temporal-contextual gap in the available field of research on the EHEA by covering the recent period post-2020. The state of affairs post-2020 is of a special interest here because in addition to the change of European geopolitics in 2020 following the end of the Brexit transitional period, 2020 was the deadline for the achievement of a 'fully-functioning EHEA' (EHEA, 2024) and planning further work, as well as following the launch of a full-scale war against Ukraine by Russia, which is a significant political phenomenon in Europe. This first collective case study makes an essential contribution to the scholarship about the EHEA by advancing our limited knowledge about its initiators and Europeanisation in the early 2020s.

3.5 Conclusion

This chapter has mapped the landscape of existing research into the European project and the EHEA. This literature review has explored key debates around the borders of the European project, analysed Europe as a space of meaning, the balance between unity and diversity in it and its evolving mission. The literature review above has also delved into the relationship between the European project and the EHEA, highlighting how the EHEA has been built and what is known to date about its role in crafting the European project. This chapter has also pointed out a few major gaps in the reviewed scholarship. These overlapping gaps are related to the role of European HE represented by EHEA initiatives in understanding the evolving mission of the European project in the early 2020s era.

References

Abélès, M. (2020). Virtual Europe. In I. Bellier & T. M. Wilson (Eds.), *An anthropology of the European Union* (pp. 31–52). Routledge.

Anderson, B. (1983). *Imagined communities: Reflections on the origin and spread of nationalism*. Verson. ISBN-10 1844670864.

Antoniolli, L. (2006). Legal education in Italy and the Bologna Process. *European Journal of Legal Education, 3*(2), 143–145.

Antonsich, M. (2008). EUropean attachment and meanings of EUrope. A qualitative study in the EU-15. *Political Geography, 27*(6), 691–710. https://doi.org/10.1016/j.polgeo.2008.07.004

Bebler, A. (2015). Peace in Europe and the Nobel Peace Prize. *Israel Journal of Foreign Affairs, 7*(3), 115–125. https://doi.org/10.1080/23739770.2013.11446571

Bellier, I., & Wilson, T. M. (EDs.). (2020). Building, imagining and experiencing Europe: Institutions and identities in the European Union. In *An anthropology of the European Union* (pp. 1–27). Routledge.

Clycq, N. (2021). Rethinking unity in diversity: The potential of European identity in rapidly diversifying societies. *Innovation: The European Journal of Social Science Research, 34*(1), 14–27. https://doi.org/10.1080/13511610.2020.1752157

Corbett, A. (2005). *Universities and the Europe of knowledge – Ideas, institutions and policy entrepreneurship in European Union higher education policy, 1955–2005*. Palgrave Macmillan. https://doi.org/10.1057/9780230286467

Datler, G., Roessel, J., & Schroedter, J. H. (2021). What is Europe? The meaning of Europe in different social contexts in Switzerland. *Swiss Political Science Review, 27*(2), 390–411. https://doi.org/10.1111/spsr.12460

Dedman, M. (2009). *The origins & development of the European Union 1945-2008: A history of European integration*. Routledge. https://doi.org/10.4324/9780203873618

Derrida, J. (1992). *The other heading: Reflections on today's Europe*. Indiana University Press. ISBN-10 0253316936.

Diogo, S. (2020). Looking back in anger? Putting in perspective the implementation of the Bologna Process in Finnish and Portuguese higher education systems. *European Journal of Cultural and Political Sociology, 7*(2), 123–149. https://doi.org/10.1080/23254823.2019.1694420

EC. (2020). Education in the EU: European education area. https://ec.europa.eu/education/education-in-the-eu/european-education-area_en. Accessed on November 19, 2023.

EHEA. (2024). How does the Bologna Process work. https://ehea.info/page-how-does-the-bologna-process-work. Accessed July 2, 2024.

EU. (2024). History of the EU 1990-1999. https://european-union.europa.eu/principles-countries-history/history-eu/1990-99_en. Accessed 04 21, 2024.

Ferreira, A., & Mota, L. (2019). The training of educators and teachers in Portugal in the framework of the European space for education and training (2007-2018). In R. P. Paixão, M. P. Paixão, A. G. Ferreira, A. L. Oliveira, A. M. Seixas, & C. P. Albuquerque (Eds.), *Higher education after Bologna. Challenges and perspectives.* Coimbra University Press. https://doi.org/10.14195/978-989-26-1620-9_6

Field, J. (2005). Bologna and an established system of bachelor's/master's degrees: The example of adult education in Britain. *Bildung und Erziehung, 58*(2), 207–220.

Fletcher, M. (2009). Schengen, the European court of justice and flexibility under the Lisbon treaty: Balancing the United Kingdom's 'ins' and 'outs'. *European Constitutional Law Review, 5*(1), 71–98. https://doi.org/10.1017/S1574019609000716

Follesdal, A., & Hix, S. (2006). Why there is a democratic deficit in the EU: A response to Majone and Moravcsik. *Journal of Common Market Studies, 44*(3), 533–562. https://doi.org/10.1111/j.1468-5965.2006.00650.x

Grek, S. (2008). From symbols to numbers: The shifting technologies of education governance in Europe. *European Educational Research Journal, 7*(2), 208–218. https://doi.org/10.2304/eerj.2008.7.2.208

Guth, J. (2006). The Bologna Process: The impact of higher education reform on the structure and organisation of doctoral programmes in Germany. *Higher Education in Europe, 31*(3), 327–338.

Huisman, J., & Van Der Wende, M. (2004). The EU and Bologna: Are supra- and international initiatives threatening domestic agendas? *European Journal of Education, 39*(3), 349–357. https://doi.org/10.1111/j.1465-3435.2004.00188.x

Ionela, P., & Camelia, M. (2014). Efficiency of public spending for education within the European Union in the context of the strategic framework "Education and Training 2020". *Management Strategies, 7*(4), 328–333.

Keeling, R. (2006). The Bologna Process and the Lisbon research agenda: The European Commission's expanding role in higher education discourse. *European Journal of Education, 41*(2), 203–223. https://doi.org/10.1111/j.1465-3435.2006.00256.x

Kočan, F. (2023). Europeanisation, securitisation and ontological insecurity. In *Identity, ontological security and Europeanisation in Republika Srpska* (pp. 13–72). Springer Nature Switzerland.

Kugiel, P. (2016). The refugee crisis in Europe: True causes, false solutions. *The Polish Quarterly of International Affairs, 4*, 41–59.

Kushnir, I. (2016). The role of the Bologna Process in defining Europe. *European Educational Research Journal, 15*(6), 664–675. https://doi.org/10.1177/1474904116657549

Kushnir, I. (2021). The role of the European education area in European Union integration in times of crises. *European Review, 30*(3), 301–321. https://doi.org/10.1017/S1062798721000016

Kushnir, I. (2023). Rational-choice neo-institutionalism in Europeanization in the UK and Germany: A toolkit offered by their memberships in the European Higher Education Area. *European Education, 55*(2), 61–77. https://doi.org/10.1080/10564934.2023.2226634

Kushnir, I., Eta, E. A., Mbah, M. F., & Kennedy, C. R. (2024). The orchestration of a sustainable development agenda in the European Higher Education Area.

International Journal of Sustainability in Higher Education, 25(1), 143–160. https://doi.org/10.1108/IJSHE-12-2022-0394

Kushnir, I., Kilkey, M., & Strumia, F. (2020). EU integration in the post 'migrant crisis' context: Learning new integration modes? *European Review, 28*(2), 306–324. https://doi.org/10.1017/S1062798719000425

Kushnir, I., & Yazgan, N. (2023). The politics of higher education: The European Higher Education Area through the eyes of its stakeholders in France and Italy. *Humanities and Social Sciences Communications, 10*(1), 1–11. https://doi.org/10.1057/s41599-023-02300-x

Lawn, M., & Grek, S. (2012). *Europeanising education: Governing a new policy space.* Symposium Books. https://doi.org/10.15730/books.78

Malan, T. (2004). Implementing the Bologna Process in France. *European Journal of Education, 39*(3), 289–297.

Marquand, J., & Scott, P. (2018). United Kingdom: England (and Wales up to 1999)—Aesop's hare. In *Democrats, authoritarians and the Bologna Process* (pp. 127–161). Emerald Publishing Limited.

Meacham, D., & de Warren, N. (Eds.). (2021). Europe: Myths, mappings, and meaning. In *The Routledge handbook of philosophy and Europe* (pp. 1–15). Routledge.

Moscovitz, H., & Zahavi, H. (Eds.). (2020). The Bologna Process as a foreign policy endeavour: Motivations and reactions to the externalisation of European higher education. In *The Bologna Process and its global strategy* (pp. 6–21). Routledge.

Nagy, B. (2017). *Sharing the responsibility or shifting the focus? The responses of the EU and the Visegrad countries to the post-2015 arrival of migrants and refugees.* Global Turkey in Europe working paper 17. https://www.iai.it/sites/default/files/gte_wp_17.pdf. Accessed on January 31, 2024.

Novoa, A., & Lawn, M. (2002). Introduction. In A. Novoa & M. Lawn (Eds.), *Fabricating Europe: The formation of an education space.* Kluwer Academic Publishers. https://doi.org/10.1007/0-306-47561-8

Olszewska, N. (2022). *Constructing Europe's borders. Political discourse and meaning creation in EU enlargement debates.* Doctoral dissertation. ETH Zurich.

Papatsiba, V. (2009). European higher education policy and the formation of entrepreneurial students as future European citizens. *European Educational Research Journal, 8*(2), 189–203. https://doi.org/10.2304/eerj.2009.8.2.189

Pastore, F., & Henry, G. (2016). Explaining the crisis of the European migration and asylum regime. *The International Spectator, 51*(1), 44–57. https://doi.org/10.1080/03932729.2016.1118609

Polyakova, A. (2016). The great European unravelling? *World Policy Journal, 33*(4), 68–72. https://doi.org/10.1215/07402775-3813051

Powell, J. J. W., & Finger, C. (2013). The Bologna Process's model of mobility in Europe: The relationship of its spatial and social dimensions. *European Educational Research Journal, 12*(2), 270. https://doi.org/10.2304/eerj.2013.12.2.270

Reichert, S. (2010). The intended and unintended effects of the Bologna reforms. *Higher Education Management and Policy, 22*(1), 1–20. https://doi.org/10.1787/17269822

Robertson, S. (2008). 'Europe/Asia' regionalism, higher education and the production of world order. *Policy Futures in Education, 6*(6), 718–729. https://doi.org/10.2304/pfie.2008.6.6.718

Robertson, S., de Azevedo, M., & Dale, R. (2016). Higher education, the EU and the cultural political economy of regionalism. In S. L. Robertson, K. Olds, R. Dale, & Q. A. Dang (Eds.), *Global regionalisms and higher education* (pp. 24–48). Edward Elgar Publishing. ISBN-10 1784712345.

Sassatelli, M. (2021). Europe's cosmopolitan identity. Images of unity in diversity in the euro. In *Images of Europe: The union between federation and separation* (pp. 195–208). Springer International Publishing.

Sayer, D. (2017). White riot—Brexit, Trump, and post-factual politics. *Journal of Historical Sociology*, *30*(1), 92–106. https://doi.org/10.1111/johs.12153

Scott, P. (2012). Going beyond Bologna: Issues and themes. In A. Curaj, P. Scott, L. Vlasceanu, & L. Wilson (Eds.), *European higher education at the crossroads: Between the Bologna Process and national reforms*. Springer. https://doi.org/10.1007/978-94-007-3937-6

Taggart, P., & Szczerbiak, A. (2018). Putting Brexit into perspective: The effect of the Eurozone and migration crises and Brexit on Euroscepticism in European states. *Journal of European Public Policy*, *25*(8), 1194–1214. https://doi.org/10.1080/13501763.2018.1467955

Teichler, U. (2012). International student mobility and the Bologna Process. *Research in Comparative and International Education*, *7*(1), 34. https://doi.org/10.2304/rcie.2012.7.1.34

Veiga, A. (2012). Bologna 2010. The moment of truth? *European Journal of Education*, *47*(3), 378–391. https://doi.org/10.1111/j.1465-3435.2012.01532.x

Veiga, A. (2023). Unthinking the European Higher Education Area: Differentiated integration and Bologna's different configurations. In *Globalizing higher education and strengthening the European spirit* (pp. 93–110). Routledge.

Veiga, A., Magalhaes, A., & Amaral, A. (2015). Differentiated integration and the Bologna Process. *Journal of Contemporary European Research*, *11*(1), 84–102.

Vögtle, E. M. (2014). *Higher education policy convergence and the Bologna Process: A cross-national study*. Palgrave Macmillan. https://doi.org/10.1057/9781137412799

Vögtle, E. M., & Martens, K. (2014). The Bologna Process as a template for transnational policy coordination. *Policy Studies*, *35*(3), 246–263. https://doi.org/10.1080/01442872.2013.875147

Walters, W. (2009). Europe's borders. In C. Rumford (Ed.), *Sage handbook of European studies*. SAGE. https://doi.org/10.4135/9780857021045

Weiss, J., & Egea-Cortines, M. (2008). Teaching applied genetics and molecular biology to agriculture engineers. Application of the European credit transfer system. *European Journal of Engineering Education*, *33*(1), 59–66. https://doi.org/10.1080/03043790701746256

Zahavi, H., & Friedman, Y. (2019). The Bologna Process: An international higher education regime. *European Journal of Higher Education*, *9*(1), 23–39. https://doi.org/10.1080/21568235.2018.1561314

Chapter 4

Germany's Membership in the European Higher Education Area: Leading Europe

Authored by Iryna Kushnir

Abstract

This chapter places Germany, as one of the four founders of the European Higher Education Area (EHEA), at the centre of attention and analyses its Bologna stakeholders' perspectives on the role of European higher education (HE) represented by the case of the EHEA in the evolving mission of the European project, which is seen here as the Europeanisation project transcending the borders of the EU. The period of the early 2020s is the focus here. The analysis rests on the ideas of neo-institutionalism and is based on in-depth interviews with key German EHEA-related stakeholders and a selection of key official communications. The findings demonstrate that German Bologna stakeholders view Germany's EHEA membership largely as a tool for generating and maintaining political stability in the European region, and Germany takes an active leading role in this process.

Keywords: Germany; Bologna Process; European Higher Education Area; EHEA; Europeanisation; Europe; neo-institutionalism; policy; politics

4.1 Introduction

This is the first of the four chapters presenting the data from the project reported in this book. This chapter places Germany, as one of the four founders of the European Higher Education Area (EHEA), at the centre of attention and analyses its Bologna stakeholders' perspectives on the role of European higher education (HE) represented by the case of the EHEA in the evolving mission of the European project in the early 2020s period.[1]

The neo-institutionalist approach which frames the analysis in this book was spelled out in Chapter 2. The gaps in prior relevant research that this chapter addresses, collectively with other chapters which present data from the case studies, and the methodological considerations of the project that informs this chapter were detailed in Chapter 1. To remind, the discussion of the German case here relies on a thematic analysis of eight in-depth semi-structured interviews with an opportunistic/snowball sample of key German Bologna stakeholders and 10 of their official communications.[2] The interviewees include three key HE actors who did not wish to reveal their organisational affiliation as well as representatives from the Federal Ministry of Education and Research in Germany, German Rectors' Conference, Free Association of Students' Unions (FZS), Erasmus+ National Agency, DAAD and the Education and Science Workers' Union (GEW).

The findings presented in this chapter demonstrate that German Bologna stakeholders view Germany's EHEA membership largely as a tool for generating and maintaining political stability in the European region, and Germany takes an active leading role in this process. This chapter continues by contextualising some key recent developments in German politics, which is then followed by a review of literature on the Bologna Process (BP) in Germany and outlining and discussing key findings from the empirical part of the study.

4.2 Recent Developments in German Politics

This section maps the field of available research on Germany's recent politics which, according to historical neo-institutionalism (Peters, 2019), is an essential context for the analysis of Germany's views on the role of the EHEA in the European project. This context is also key to understand the rationalisation process of German EHEA stakeholders, the analysis of which in Section 4.4 will be guided by the rational-choice strand of neo-institutionalism.

There is, of course, no consensus regarding one political direction in Germany or any country. The idea of the 'polarisation of German politics' has been slowly creeping to the forefront since the 2000s 'in an era of multiple crises' (Hutter & Weisskircher, 2023, p. 403). Germany's response to the 2015 migrant crisis, generously welcoming migrants and actively encouraging other European Union (EU)

---

[1] This chapter is derived in part from an article published in *European Education*, 28 June 2023, copyright CC BY-NC-ND 4.0, published by Routledge, Taylor & Francis Group, Informa Group Plc, available online: Kushnir, I. (2023). Rational-choice neo-institutionalism in Europeanization in the United Kingdom and Germany: A toolkit offered by their memberships in the European Higher Education Area. *European Education*, 55(2), 61–77. http://www.tandfonline.com/10.1080/10564934.2023.2226634

[2] The dataset with interview transcripts, generated and analysed during the research project that informs this book, is available in the Research Data Archive of Nottingham Trent University, at https://doi.org/10.17631/RD-2022-0001-DDOC

countries to do so through its mechanisms of influence in the EU (Ayoub, 2023), has been one of the major dividing issues in Germany. Immigration has exacerbated internal divisions in Germany (Pickel & Pickel, 2023; Reiser & Reiter, 2023) but has been one of the elements in 'a deep, triple crisis involving shaky eurozone debt, Russian aggression in the east and a sudden surge in migrants and refugees' (Matthijs, 2023, p. 135). A combination of these challenges was a fertile ground for sprouting far-right movements. These far-right movements have developed in Germany to the extent that even gave opportunities for 'intra-party conflicts over the "true" version of the shared party ideology' (Pytlas & Biehler, 2024, p. 322).

Despite the existence of Eurosceptic sentiments, such as those of the Alternative for Germany Party (AfD), 'Germany has always been a strong power in the European integration..., and few would question Germany's ideological commitment to the European project in general' (Caporaso, 2021, p. 18). Germany was even referred to as 'Europe's indispensable nation' by Radoslaw Sikorski in his November 2011 speech in Berlin who, at the time, was the Polish Minister of Foreign Affairs (Matthijs, 2023, p. 136). Its structural, institutional and ideational power has facilitated its leadership position in managing the interlocking crises in Germany and the European region, despite the so-called 'German question' of historians whether it could be considered a 'normal' country and be in the position to 'ever take on a mantle of regional or global leadership' regardless of its fascist past (Matthijs, 2023, p. 138). Germany acted as an 'enforcer-in-chief' during the Euro crisis (Matthijs, 2023, p. 144), as a 'facilitator-in-chief' during the Russian aggression crisis (Matthijs, 2023, p. 146) and a 'benefactor-in-chief' during the refugee crisis (Matthijs, 2023, p. 148).

Germany's long serving Chancellor Angela Merkel was replaced by Olaf Scholz in 2021, and despite the worries in the political circles around the continuity of Germany's politics after this change, coupled by the ongoing crises and populist gains in Germany, Germany remains EU's 'status quo power' (Becker, 2023, p. 1473). However, France's accompanying leadership in the European region (Bora & Schramm, 2023) and the smoothness of the Franco-German relationship is instrumental to Germany's effective leadership in the EU (Schramm & Krotz, 2024). The continuity of such a power configuration has been put into question, though, after the 2024 European Parliament election and the follow-up early legislative election in France which both confirmed that Macron's support had weakened and French political landscape is in chaos (Chabal & Behrent, 2024).

While the effects of this power shift in France on the Franco-German relationship is yet to be seen, the idea of Germany's undeniable leadership position in the EU is also echoed in the literature about German Europeanisation which highlights Germany's learning process in leading the way in the Europeanisation within the EU (Aggestam & Hyde-Price, 2020; Schoeller, 2019) and its assertive manner in doing so (Daehnhardt, 2022). German Europeanisation follows a bottom-up approach, given the independence that the 16 federal states have from the central government in policymaking (Kazanoğlu, 2021).

4.3 The BP in Germany

HE reforms in Germany in the context of its membership in the EHEA cannot be analysed without acknowledging that the education system in Germany is federalised, which prompts us to assume a degree of policy fragmentation in the implementation of education reforms in Germany. However, despite this federalism, the EHEA-related reforms in Germany have been more successful than any prior reforms due to effective soft governance which is part and parcel of the BP (Toens, 2009). The added incentive of Germany to exert its soft power in the European region through the EHEA to promote cooperation in the region has also helped the BP gain momentum in Germany (Kushnir, 2023).

The focus on the impact of the BP in Germany has been the most prevalent in relevant scholarship. There is a range of studies which highlight structural adaptations of Germany to the Bologna action points in specific areas of studies such as legal (Bücker & Woodruff, 2008; Riedel, 2005; Terry, 2019), nursing (Hensen, 2010; Taneva et al., 2023) and teacher training education (Kless & Pfeiffer, 2013). There are also studies about the impact of the BP on the German HE system in general. This is related to, for example, the success of the universities of applied sciences in Germany in their implementation of the BP (Teuscher, 2023), as well as progress towards measuring students' workload and understanding HE quality (De Rudder, 2010; Turner, 2019; Winkel, 2010) across German universities. Aside from this, scholarship discusses the impact of the BP on such specific aspects of German HE as doctoral education (Guth, 2006; Kehm, 2023) and student mobility (Gareis & Broekel, 2022). It is also worth highlighting a separate body of scholarship where the impact of the BP on the German HE is one of a range of case studies in focus or where BP's impact on Germany is mentioned in passing, such as in Dobbins et al. (2023), Teichler (2023), Zgaga (2023) and Lohse (2024).

Given the all-encompassing nature of the BP (Dobbins & Knill, 2009) and, more importantly, a degree of fatigue around the long and persistent discussions about it in the academic circles (Gareis & Broekel, 2022; Mendick & Peters, 2022; Pires Pereira et al., 2021), there is a plethora or recent studies about HE in Germany which touch on the ideas of the BP but do not make any explicit references to it or Germany's membership in the EHEA. Such studies include the foci on student mobility in Germany (Netz & Grüttner, 2021), multilingualism in the context of the internationalisation of German HE (Bradlaw et al., 2024), continuity in HE reforms (Rohs et al., 2023) and graduate employability (Petzold, 2021).

The range of overlapping gaps in prior relevant research was detailed in Chapters 1 and 3. However, it is worth mentioning again that with regard to the German case in particular, the above literature review has demonstrated that the state of affairs with respect to Germany's membership in the EHEA after 2020 has not been the focus of attention, Germany has not been studied as a founder of the EHEA along with the other three founders by other scholars and the link of Germany's EHEA membership and wider politics remains an under-researched area.

4.4 Germany's Membership in the EHEA as a Channel for Its Soft Power in Promoting Stability in the European Region

The analysis of the interviews and official communications from key Bologna stakeholders in Germany has shed light on their vision of the role of HE in Europe in the recent context. This section presents key findings and discusses them in light of the theoretical and empirical literature outlined in the earlier chapters of this book. These findings focus on the German stakeholders' rationalisation of Germany's EHEA membership as a tool for generating and maintaining political stability in the region, and their perspectives on how Germany has been taking an active leading role in this process.

Germany plays an active role in the EHEA, according to the interviews conducted, which also resonates with the literature review presented above (e.g. Kushnir, 2023; Toens, 2009). What this literature does not address and what this study provides is an account of how the rationale for Germany's membership in the EHEA is negotiated by key Bologna stakeholders. Another point that this literature does not address and that this study provides is how Germany's membership in the EHEA fits with Germany's wider politics. This chapter highlights that while Germany is not the same kind of driver of the EHEA as it used to be in the past when work on building the EHEA started in 1998, Germany still leads on many aspects of EHEA's work, and all of German Bologna stakeholders express Germany's sense of responsibility for the stability in Europe and the development of European HE. What concerns HE, key German Bologna stakeholders' rationales for actively supporting Germany's active role in the EHEA are as follows. One of the key rationales is cooperation in HE with the focus not only on harmonising HE structures but more importantly the values of democracy. The other rationale for Germany's membership in the EHEA is benefit-drawing for the improvement of German HE and economy. Crucially, in addition to these specifically HE-related incentives, there are two wider incentives, which are emphasised more by the interviewees, related to promoting political stability and security in the European region.

The thematic analysis has revealed a prominent theme of Germany's sense of responsibility for promoting the politics of cooperation and peace-keeping in the European region and around it, which is partly exercised through its work in the EHEA. The representatives from the Bologna stakeholders in Germany were unanimous on this. It is striking to see how Bologna stakeholders use this reason to reinforce the importance of their commitment to the EHEA:

> ...we think that the EHEA can facilitate... exchanges of opinions, of science. And let people meet with each other, so that they can't imagine anymore to have war with each other. In a way, it is more than just education. It's also a peace policy if you want... [the BP is] about unity... at least we want to reach that we don't have war against each other. That we talk to each other, that we understand each other. And we think that the EHEA can facilitate that process. (B1, a representative from the Federal Ministry of Education and Research)

The link between education and peace is timely in the context of the invasion of Ukraine, which is what the interviewee above implied, although the interview took place just before the full-scale attack on Ukraine was launched in February 2022. The ideas expressed remain relevant as the political strategic significance of being a member of the EHEA remains the same for Germany:

> ...it is still the dialogue with Eastern Europe, especially the Russia-influenced countries that were part of the Soviet Union before... So, this is still one strategic point. The other is, of course, to have a link with Western countries, that are not parties in the EU, but that are traditionally strong partners of Germany, like Turkey, Norway, UK, Switzerland. (B1, a representative from the Federal Ministry of Education and Research)

Germany's Bologna stakeholders' choice to view and use Germany's EHEA's membership as a tool for enacting Germany's sense of responsibility for developing cooperation and friendship in the European region is in line with the literature on Germany's leading role specifically in the EU (Aggestam & Hyde-Price, 2020; Becker, 2023; Daehnhardt, 2022). While this literature is limited to the discussions of the EU, the ethos of Germany's aspiration to support Europeanisation in the region, evident from this literature, runs in parallel with the findings from this project on Germany's utilisation of its EHEA membership as a way to promote Europeanisation. Although in the EHEA's case, Germany's Europeanisation acquires a new meaning – wider cooperation and a friendship-zone generation, and a clear bridge between developments in HE cooperation and wider politics. Education can never be neutral – it is always political (Marshall & Scribner, 1991). Thus, it is not surprising that there is a mutually shaping relationship between HE and the context in which it operates, as discussed extensively by the representatives from key Bologna stakeholders in Germany as well as evident in their official communications. For example, the EHEA is explicitly mentioned in *the Internationalisation Strategy* for Germany (Federal Ministry of Education and Research, 2017, p. 64), emphasising academic mobility and resulting cooperation in the European region as the drivers of 'stability and peace in the regions involved'.

The potential for the EHEA to be a platform for Germany's stability-inspired soft power in the European region has, arguably, increased recently. Apparently, the EHEA had lost its momentum (Gareis & Broekel, 2022; Mendick & Peters, 2022; Pires Pereira et al., 2023), but the new war in the European region has reignited the need not to lose this platform for promoting cooperation:

> The relevance for EHEA has been changing over the years... And long before war in Ukraine, I often thought that it would be almost impossible to get the European Higher Education Area going nowadays. (B4, a representative from the Rectors' Conference in Germany)

The most turbulent times since WWII that have arrived to Europe with the attack on Ukraine and other crises that have recently occurred have inspired another aspect of Germany's wider politics of cooperation using its EHEA membership as a tool for promoting the politics of friendship and creating a ring of friends specifically around Germany – for Germany's safety:

> We are located in the middle of Europe, and international cooperation is becoming more important every year. (B2, a key HE actor in Germany)

What concerns HE, in particular, Bologna stakeholders in Germany choose to be active in the EHEA to drive cooperation in HE in the region with the new emphasis not only on the structural aspects of HE, which is the focus of prior literature on the topic (e.g. Gareis & Broekel, 2022; Turner, 2019), but more importantly, the values of democracy, academic freedom and integrity:

> ...what used to be the core of Bologna: increasing mobility, introducing study cycles... in that sense Bologna has become less important. It is becoming more important in other regards and we're coming to that: fundamental values, academic freedom, and now, of course, the war on Ukraine – we would rather see the importance of the Bologna Process in this area now as a forum for exchange. (B4, a representative from the Rectors' Conference in Germany)

Lastly, it is not surprising that Germany, similarly to other countries, would have some self-related interests associated specifically to HE while pursuing the EHEA, such as using the EHEA membership to improve German HE specifically and, as a consequence, its economy:

> ...it's also easier, when you have a problem, to call someone in another country and ask him, how do you solve the problem? (B1, a representative from the Federal Ministry of Education and Research in Germany)

> Europeanisation is very important for Germany on an economic level. That's also an education thing, that's why there's a lot of interest... they [central government] were like, we're going to have this huge European thing [the BP] and if we don't do this all together, then we are going to be left behind. And so, the whole process [the BP] was used to give motivation to the federal ministers to really do some reforms. (B5, a representative from the Free Association of Students' Unions)

While benefit-drawing for HE improvement through implementing different action points of the BP is a typical theme in prior literature on the BP in Germany (e.g. Hüther & Krücken, 2018; Turner, 2019), viewing this as part of wider economic benefits and, more importantly, a method of governance shift has not been a focus in the literature. The last quote above is a powerful example of how Germany's EHEA membership has been used by the central government bodies in Germany as a power tool for them to establish a form of control through coordinating the work of the independent federal ministries in the area of HE. The BP is also acknowledged as a driver for 'promoting higher education reform in Germany' on the national level in the press release of the Federal Ministry of Education and Research (2021), although the gravity of what is meant in this official communication can only be realised when put in the context of the discussion with the interviewee mentioned above. The scope of these coordinated and harmonised national reforms had not previously been possible in the fragmented policy context of German federalism (Toens, 2009).

4.5 Conclusion

Chapter 4 has placed Germany in the spotlight, with it serving as the first of the four elements of the collective case study of the EHEA's founders' perspectives on the role of European HE, represented by the EHEA initiatives, in our understanding of the evolving European project's mission in the early 2020s. Chapter 4 has contextualised recent political developments in Germany and provided an outline of the literature on the BP in Germany before presenting and discussing key findings. The data have demonstrated that German EHEA-related stakeholders have been viewing Germany's EHEA membership as a tool for supporting political stability in the European region. Importantly, Germany has been taking an active leading role in this process. The findings presented in this chapter are further discussed in relation to the findings from the remaining case studies in Chapter 8.

References

Aggestam, L., & Hyde-Price, A. (2020). Learning to lead? Germany and the leadership paradox in EU foreign policy. *German Politics, 29*(1), 8–24.

Ayoub, M. A. (2023). Understanding Germany's response to the 2015 refugee crisis. *Review of Economics and Political Science, 8*(6), 577–604.

Becker, P. (2023). Germany as the European Union's status quo power? Continuity and change in the shadow of the Covid-19 pandemic. *Journal of European Public Policy, 30*(8), 1473–1493.

Bora, S. I., & Schramm, L. (2023). Toward a more 'sovereign' Europe? Domestic, bilateral, and European factors to explain France's (growing) influence on EU politics, 2017–2022. *French Politics, 21*(1), 3–24.

Bradlaw, C., Hufeisen, B., & Nölle-Becker, S. (2024). The concept of functional multilingualism in the context of internationalisation at German universities. In D. Gabryś-Barker & E. Vetter (Eds.), *Modern approaches to researching multilingualism: Studies in honour of Larissa Aronin* (pp. 61–80). Springer Nature Switzerland.

Bücker, A., & Woodruff, W. A. (2008). The Bologna Process and German legal education: Developing professional competence through clinical experiences. *German Law Journal*, *9*(5), 575–618.

Caporaso, J. A. (2021). Germany and the eurozone crisis: Power, dominance, and hegemony. In M. Kim & J. Caporaso (Eds.), *Power relations and comparative regionalism* (pp. 18–43). Routledge.

Chabal, E., & Behrent, M. C. (2024). The deluge: France's 2024 legislative elections. *Modern and Contemporary France*, *32*(3), 329–337. https://doi.org/10.1080/09639489.2024.2381787

Daehnhardt, P. (2022). Germany in the EU: An assertive Status Quo power? In K. Larres, H. Moroff, & R. Wittlinger (Eds.), *The Oxford handbook of German politics*. Oxford University Press.

De Rudder, H. (2010). Mission accomplished? Which mission? The "Bologna Process"—A view from Germany. *Higher Education Review*, *43*(1), 3–20.

Dobbins, M., & Knill, C. (2009). Higher education policies in Central and Eastern Europe: Convergence toward a common model? *Governance*, *22*(3), 397–430.

Dobbins, M., Martens, K., Niemann, D., & Vögtle, E. M. (2023). The Bologna Process as a multidimensional architecture of policy diffusion in Western Europe. In J. Jungblut, M. Maltais, E. C. Ness, & D. Rexe (Eds.), *Comparative higher education politics: Policymaking in North America and Western Europe* (pp. 427–453). Springer International Publishing.

Federal Ministry of Education and Research. (2017). Internationalisation of education, science and research. https://www.bmbf.de/SharedDocs/Publikationen/de/bmbf/FS/31286_Internationalisierungsstrategie_en.pdf?__blob=publicationFile&v=3. Accessed on October 17, 2022.

Federal Ministry of Education and Research in Germany. (2021, 10 March). *Bologna report in the Cabinet*. https://www.bundesregierung.de/breg-en/news/bologna-process-1875358. Accessed on October 17, 2022.

Gareis, P., & Broekel, T. (2022). The spatial patterns of student mobility before, during and after the Bologna Process in Germany. *Tijdschrift voor Economische en Sociale Geografie*, *113*(3), 290–309.

Guth, J. (2006). The Bologna Process: The impact of higher education reform on the structure and organisation of doctoral programmes in Germany. *Higher Education in Europe*, *31*(3), 327–338.

Hensen, P. (2010). The "Bologna Process" in European Higher Education: Impact of bachelor's and master's degrees on German medical education. *Teaching and Learning in Medicine*, *22*(2), 142–147.

Hüther, O., & Krücken, G. (2018). *Higher education in Germany – Recent developments in an international perspective* (Vol. 49). Springer International Publishing.

Hutter, S., & Weisskircher, M. (2023). New contentious politics. Civil society, social movements, and the polarisation of German politics. *German Politics*, *32*(3), 403–419.

Kazanoğlu, N. (2021). *The politics of Europeanisation: Work and family life reconciliation policy*. Routledge.

Kehm, B. M. (2023). International developments in doctoral education. Case study: Germany. *Innovations in Education & Teaching International*, *60*(5), 668–676.

Kless, E., & Pfeiffer, A. (2013). The Bologna Process and its changes for the teacher education in Rhineland-Palatinate, Germany–media-education-online as an innovative example for statewide cooperation of universities. *International Journal of Innovation and Learning*, *13*(2), 218–232.

Kushnir, I. (2023). Rational-choice neo-institutionalism in Europeanization in the UK and Germany: A toolkit offered by their memberships in the European Higher Education Area. *European Education*, *55*(2), 61–77.

Lohse, A. P. (Ed.). (2024). Institutionalising European HE internationalisation. In *Higher education in an age of disruption: Comparing European internationalisation policies* (pp. 21–68). Springer Nature Switzerland.

Marshall, C., & Scribner, J. D. (1991). "It's all political" inquiry into the micropolitics of education. *Education and Urban Society*, *23*(4), 347–355. https://doi.org/10.1177/0013124591023004001

Matthijs, M. (2023). The three faces of German leadership. In *Survival 58.2* (pp. 135–154). Routledge.

Mendick, H., & Peters, A. K. (2022). How post-Bologna policies construct the purposes of higher education and students' transitions into masters programmes. *European Educational Research Journal*. https://doi.org/10.1177/14749041221076633

Netz, N., & Grüttner, M. (2021). Does the effect of studying abroad on labour income vary by graduates' social origin? Evidence from Germany. *Higher Education*, *82*(6), 1195–1217.

Peters, B. (2019). *Institutional theory in political science: The new institutionalism*. Edward Elgar Publishing. ISBN 9781786437921.

Petzold, K. (2021). Heterogeneous effects of graduates' international mobility on employers' hiring intentions—Experimental evidence from Germany. *Higher Education*, *82*(6), 1093–1118.

Pickel, S., & Pickel, G. (2023). The wall in the mind – Revisited stable differences in the political cultures of western and eastern Germany. *German Politics*, *32*(1), 20–42.

Pires Pereira, Í. S., Fernandes, E. L., Braga, A. C., & Flores, M. A. (2023). Initial teacher education after the Bologna Process. Possibilities and challenges for a renewed scholarship of teaching and learning. *European Journal of Teacher Education*, *46*(2), 1–29. https://doi.org/10.1080/02619768.2020.1867977

Pires Pereira, Í. S., Fernandes, E. L., Braga, A. C., & Flores, M. A. (2021). Initial teacher education after the Bologna Process. Possibilities and challenges for a renewed scholarship of teaching and learning. *European Journal of Teacher Education*, *44*, 1–29.

Pytlas, B., & Biehler, J. (2024). The AfD within the AfD: Radical right intra-party competition and ideational change. *Government and Opposition*, *59*(2), 322–340.

Reiser, M., & Reiter, R. (2023). A (new) east–west-divide? Representative democracy in Germany 30 years after unification. *German Politics*, *32*(1), 1–19.

Riedel, J. (2005). The Bologna Process and its relevance for legal education in Germany. *European Journal of Legal Education*, *2*(1), 59–62.

Rohs, M., Heinbach, G., & Tokarski, B. M. (2023). Governance of university continuing education in Germany. A scoping review of research in a game-changing area. *Zeitschrift für Weiterbildungsforschung*, *46*(1), 25–42.

Schoeller, M. G. (2019). *Leadership in the eurozone: The role of Germany and EU institutions*. Palgrave Macmillan.

Schramm, L., & Krotz, U. (2024). Leadership in European crisis politics: France, Germany, and the difficult quest for regional stabilization and integration. *Journal of European Public Policy*, *31*(5), 1153–1178.

Taneva, D., Paskaleva, D., & Gyurova-Kancheva, V. (2023). Nursing education in some European Higher Education Area (EHEA) member countries: A comparative analysis. *Iranian Journal of Public Health*, *52*(7), 1418.

Teichler, U. (2023). Bologna and student mobility: A fuzzy relationship. In C. Dienel (Ed.), *Globalizing higher education and strengthening the European spirit* (pp. 27–47). Routledge.

Terry, L. (2019). Living with the Bologna Process: Recommendations to the German legal education community from a U.S. perspective. *German Law Journal*, *7*(11), 863–905. https://doi.org/10.1017/S2071832200005186

Teuscher, M. (2023). Universities of applied sciences in Germany: The winners of "Bologna"? In *Globalizing higher education and strengthening the European spirit* (pp. 114–123). Routledge.

Toens, K. (2009). The Bologna Process in German educational federalism: State strategies, policy fragmentation and interest mediation. *German Politics*, *18*(2), 246–264.

Turner, G. (2019). How the Bologna Process has affected the German university system. *Innovation: The European Journal of Social Science Research*, *32*(4), 513–515.

Winkel, O. (2010). Higher education reform in Germany: How the aims of the Bologna Process can be simultaneously supported and missed. *International Journal of Educational Management*, *24*(4), 303–313.

Zgaga, P. (2023). The Bologna Process in a global setting: Twenty years later. In C. Dienel (Ed.), *Globalizing higher education and strengthening the European spirit* (pp. 48–62). Routledge.

Chapter 5

France's Membership in the European Higher Education Area: (Still) 'Moderating' the Leading of Europe

Authored by Iryna Kushnir and Nuve Yazgan

Abstract

This chapter presents an analysis of the politics of French stakeholders' choice to be in and develop the European Higher Education Area (EHEA) and the significance of this for the European project, which has been emerging as a phenomenon wider than the EU itself. Similarly to the previous chapter, empirical research here is informed by neo-institutionalism and is based on in-depth interviews with key French stakeholders in the Bologna Process and their key official communications on the topic. The findings demonstrate that France appears to support Germany's leading position in the Europeanisation in the region. Evidently, French EHEA stakeholders choose to position France as a 'moderator' country in the Europeanisation process in the European region in the early 2020s, with the EHEA being a forum for EHEA members' cooperation in higher education and wider political diplomacy.

Keywords: France European Higher Education Area; Europe; Bologna Process; politics; policy

5.1 Introduction

This chapter presents the second of the four elements of the collective case study of European Higher Education Area (EHEA) founders' perspectives on the role of European cooperation in higher education (HE) in the evolving mission of the European project in the early 2020s. France is the focus in this chapter.

European Cooperation in Higher Education, 57–71
Copyright © 2025 Iryna Kushnir and Nuve Yazgan.
Published by Emerald Publishing Limited. This work is published under the Creative Commons Attribution (CC BY 4.0) licence. Anyone may reproduce, distribute, translate and create derivative works of this work (for both commercial and non-commercial purposes), subject to full attribution to the original publication and authors. The full terms of this licence may be seen at http://creativecommons.org/licences/by/4.0/legalcode
doi:10.1108/978-1-83753-516-320251013

The neo-institutionalist approach which informs the analysis in this book was spelled out in Chapter 2. The gaps in prior relevant scholarship that this chapter contributes to addressing and the details of the methodological decisions underpinning the project reported in this book were presented in the introductory chapter. However, it is worth reminding here that the analysis of the French case relies on four in-depth semi-structured elite interviews with an opportunistic/snowball sample of key Bologna stakeholders in France, as well as 25 of their official communications.[1] The interviewees include a French expert in the Bologna Process (BP) and representatives from ENIC-NARIC France, the Assembly of Directors of University Institutes of Technology (ADIUT), a national student organisation (FAGE).

This chapter proceeds with outlining recent developments in French politics as an essential context for the analysis later in the chapter. This is then followed by the review of literature on the BP in France before key findings are presented regarding French EHEA stakeholders' perspectives on the role of HE in Europe in the early 2020s period.

5.2 Recent Developments in French Politics

The following literature review maps the field of available research on recent state of affairs and challenges in French politics and the links that these developments have with Europeanisation and, in particular, Franco-German relations as a key aspect of French external relations. This background information is key to understand the developments with regard to the French membership in the EHEA later, following the logic of the historical strand of neo-institutionalism.

5.2.1 Crises as a Context

French politics has undergone a range of defining developments in the recent years which have been facilitated by turbulent global sociopolitical phenomena. These developments have been shaped by migration flows, climate change, protest movements, the COVID-19 pandemic and associated evolving French politics during Macron's Presidency since 2017. Many of these phenomena are not exclusive to France as they have an impact on the European region and beyond. Therefore, it is not possible to separate these from the Europeanisation trends in France. In recent years, there has been an increasing amount of literature on immigration flow into France and the EU (European Union).

Immigration has been a divisive matter in the realm of French politics (Ostermann & Stahl, 2022). It entered the political agenda a few years ago, with the post-2015 'migrant crisis' due to a dramatic increase in border crossings resulting from conflicts in Syria and Afghanistan (Kushnir et al., 2020). According to Vertier et al. (2023), France received the influx of asylum seekers

---

[1]The dataset with interview transcripts, generated and analysed during the research project that informs this book, is available in the Research Data Archive of Nottingham Trent University, at https://doi.org/10.17631/RD-2022-0001-DDOC.

similar to some first-entry European countries, such as Greece and Italy. The asylum seekers coming to France settled in Calais in North France, and by October 2016, an unauthorised camp with a population of 6,400 residents had emerged. However, it was subsequently shut down by the government, and the migrants were dispersed to different regions across the country. Vertier et al. (2023) examine the relationship between the relocation of these migrants and extreme voting patterns in France. They explore the impact of the dismantling of the migrant camp in Calais on voters' political attitudes and electoral behaviour. They argue that the dismantling of the camp heightened public concern about immigration and led to an increase in the support for far-right anti-migration political parties. Similar to other EU countries, French politics has been challenged by extreme powers. For instance, there are similarities of immigration attitudes of people who vote for far-right parties: French Rassemblement (RN) national and the German Alternative for Germany (AfD) (Ostermann & Stahl, 2022). Another challenge in French politics has been recent protest movements (Duyvendak, 2019; Bourdin & Torre, 2023). They are related to economic concerns and managing other challenging influences of globalisation. France has experienced social unrest, particularly with the Yellow Vest movement that emerged in 2018. The movement highlighted issues of economic inequality, dissatisfaction with government policies and the demands for greater social justice (Jetten et al., 2020). This unrest can also be associated with the environmental politics in France. There has been a growing emphasis on sustainability, the utilisation of renewable energy sources and the reduction of carbon emissions in the country. Public trust in institutions and political actors play a crucial role in shaping attitudes towards climate policies in France (Douenne & Fabre, 2020). Scepticism towards government effectiveness and concerns about the transparency and fairness of policy implementation can hinder public support for climate measures. The protests underscore the need for effective communication, addressing economic and social considerations and building trust in order to garner broader support for climate action in France. Another protest movement emerged in 2023 due to pension reform package introduced by President Macron. Large-scale strikes and demonstrations were held to oppose government plans to reform the pension system, with concerns over the potential impact on retirement age and benefits (Vail et al., 2023).

Apart from these challenges in France, the management of the COVID-19 pandemic has been a significant issue related to managing vaccinations rates and balancing public health with freedoms. French public's approval of relevant COVID-19 safety measures depended strongly on their low level of trust in the national leaders (Altiparmakis et al., 2021). The vaccination campaign, in particular, became politicised. Compared to the supporters of the political centre, the supporters of the far-left and green parties were more likely to be opposed to mandatory COVID-19 vaccine (Gagneux-Brunon et al., 2022) – a different trend to the right-wing vaccine hesitancy in other countries such as the United States (Carpiano et al., 2023). However, France overall had a high prevalence of vaccine hesitancy (Bajos et al., 2022).

The COVID-19 crisis and unidentical government reactions to the pandemic across the EU have further underscored the need for European solidarity, and

Macron was at the forefront of pushing for coordinated responses from the EU countries. He called for joint EU efforts to address the economic impact of the pandemic, including the issuance of shared debt through the EU Recovery Fund. Macron saw the crisis as an opportunity to strengthen European cooperation and build a more resilient and socially oriented Europe (Clegg, 2022). Evidently, the pandemic reinforced the importance of European solidarity, with President Macron taking a leading role along with Germany in advocating for coordinated European responses (Kempin, 2021).

The incrementally growing weight of the multiple and interlocking crises in France has significantly challenged the support for Macron which has led to a political turmoil in France. Macron called snap parliamentary elections in June 2024 in the wake of a big victory for his rival Marine Le Pen's National Rally party in the 2024 European Parliament vote. Chabal and Behrent (2024, p. 330) summarise these developments by stating that 'Macron successfully provoked a political earthquake, but he has not been able to control the new political landscape he created.' This is because while the far-right National Rally failed to secure the most seats in the snap legislative elections, they set sight on the 2027 presidential vote, the left-wing New Popular Front coalition came first, with Macron's centrist coalition coming in second. President Macron has refused to name Lucie Castets from the New Popular Front as Prime Minister, which had led to a political crisis (BBC, 2024). At the time of writing this chapter, the country is still stuck in a political standoff. The examples of the crises in the recent years briefly discussed above sparked debates about the role of the EU in French politics. An increasing influx of immigrants has brought forward the debates on national identity, immigration policies and the rise of far-right populism in France (Ostermann & Stahl, 2022). Protest movements highlighted deep divisions within French society and fuelled debates about income inequality, taxation and the role of the state (Bourdin & Torre, 2023). The pandemic highlighted the strengths and weaknesses of the French healthcare system and exacerbated discussions on public trust in the political leaders in France (Brouard et al., 2020). Overall, these crises contributed to uncertainty and prevented a smooth implementation of French reform agendas.

5.2.2 The Evolution of European Politics in France and Macron's Leadership

The crises mentioned above have significantly influenced the development of France's Europeanisation. During the formation of the EU, France maintained its significant role, although not as dominant as Germany, which emerged as the forefront leader of the EU (Aggestam & Hyde-Price, 2020). However, both France and Germany played a crucial role in the establishment of a unified Europe following World War II (Sutton, 2007). The deep-rooted bilateral relationship between the two countries has allowed them to collectively influence the shaping of Europe, according to Krotz and Schild (2013). They emphasised the importance of such factors as adaptability in the close relationship between France and Germany, in spite of some inherent differences in their political aims, such as in the case of their stances on international affairs and the pressures exerted by policy stakeholders within their nations.

In the context of France's efforts to collaborate with Germany in driving European integration, France itself has undergone Europeanisation as a result of the evolving nature of European integration since the 1950s. Europeanisation is explained by Ladrech (1994, p. 69) as 'an incremental process re-orienting the direction and shape of politics to the degree that political and economic dynamics of the EU become part of the organisational logic of national politics and policy-making.'

During the 1980s, domestic actors in France within the Fifth Republic, that is the current republican system of government in France, established in 1958, perceived European integration as institutional changes to be resisted (Ladrech, 1994). French authorities viewed European integration as a strategy to constrain German influence following World War II since Germany has consolidated its economic power (Giurlando, 2021). The imbalance between France and Germany became more pronounced following the reunification of Germany and the expansion of the EU to include Central and Eastern European countries (Steible et al., 2022). Nevertheless, France remained a key player within the EU but not as strong of a player as in the case of Germany that emerged as a supreme leader of the EU. For instance, France's rejection of the EU's constitutional treaty in the 2005 referendum illustrated France's so-called lukewarm leadership role in the EU (Sutton, 2007). However, regardless of some of such Euro-sceptic sentiments, there are plenty of strong voices in France that remain loyal to sustaining France's leadership in Europe and support for Germany's efforts in this domain (Degner & Leuffen, 2019; Schild, 2013).

The start of Macron's presidency can be considered as a turning point in the Europeanisation trends in France. After taking office in 2017, Macron has been actively working towards enhancing European integration and establishing France as a significant actor in shaping the future of the EU. His election in 2017 sparked a renewed focus in France among policymakers on EU matters and a determination to revive France's involvement in European decision-making (Steible et al., 2022). Basically, Macron has been following the motto 'Make Europe Great Again', emphasising the importance of a strong and united Europe; he has been aiming to counter Euroscepticism and bolster France's position within the EU (Bouza García & Oleart, 2022, p. 272).

The nature of France's leadership role in the EU along a more powerful actor – Germany – has been the reason for summarising in the title of this chapter France's role in the EU as 'moderating the leading of Europe'. While this has been the case, the future of this position has become uncertain in the context of the most recent – at the time of writing the chapter – events in France, namely the 2024 European Parliament election and the 2024 France snap legislative election, briefly explained in the previous sub-section.

5.2.3 The Franco–German Relationship

As mentioned previously, the Franco-German partnership can be considered the motor of European integration. The below provides more details about the dynamics of this relationship. France and Germany have influenced most significant EU policies such as creating the European Council, the Single European Act and the Maastricht Treaty (Webber, 2005). The relationship between France and Germany has recently gained an even greater significance in the Brexit context (Krotz and Schramm, 2022). As the EU has been facing significant internal and external challenges, a strong partnership can be pivotal for shaping the future of European integration. Scholars argue that managing the COVID-19 pandemic has led to an improvement in the Franco-German relationship. This is due to the European Recovery initiative driven by the two countries (Steible et al., 2022). Angela Merkel and Emmanuel Macron jointly introduced a European Recovery fund to address the COVID-19 crisis. This initiative included the establishment of an ambitious recovery fund amounting to 500 billion Euros (Capati, 2024).

French leadership role in the EU along a more powerful actor – Germany – in of European integration (Aggestam and Hyde-Price, 2020) can also be traced in President Macron's putting forward the European Universities Initiative idea in 2017 in his Sorbonne speech, as part of the European Education Area. The European Universities Initiative was eventually launched by the European Commission at the end of 2018 in the Erasmus + Programme Guide for 2019. It aimed to improve strategic partnerships across EU HE institutions. President Macron's strong focus on European languages, identity and solidarity in the initiative, which is also reflected in its design, demonstrates that the European Universities Initiative primarily aims at promoting cultural integration within Europe. Importantly, in this regard, France's stance on the European University aligns with the position on European cultural integration that Germany held in the post-WWII period, both countries now envisioning the European Universities Initiative as a means to achieve the original objectives of a supranational university (Kempin, 2021).

Yet, the two countries do not necessarily share exactly the same objectives regarding global politics. Scholars highlight some differences between the two countries, particularly since Macron's presidency in 2017 which has reframed French foreign policy. For instance, differences exist in areas such as shaping transatlantic security relations, particularly with regard to NATO, as well as the economic policies of the EU (Kempin, 2021). For instance, Macron has criticised Germany's position on the Eurozone. He has consistently advocated for the abandonment of the 3% GDP debt ceiling due to it being outdated. The two countries have different perspectives on the role of NATO and dealings with Turkey (Major, 2021). Such differences in the political priorities of France and Germany have also been a precedent for some tensions between the two countries in their ongoing partnership, particularly during Macron's rule (Krotz & Schramm, 2022). The collaborative role and leadership of France and Germany, the two largest and most influential Member States of the EU, remains crucial for the future of Europe. Despite difficulties arising from different preferences, France and Germany have demonstrated joint leadership during the moments of existential threat to the EU such as during the COVID-19 pandemic (Krotz & Schramm, 2022), as well as to the security of Ukraine and the rest of Europe during Russia's attack on Ukraine (Kushnir, 2023).

5.3 The BP in France

Having discussed recent developments in French politics – the context in which French HE has been developing, it is timely to move on to the review of literature specifically about the BP in France. In the last couple of decades, the implementation of the BP and the execution of relevant changes in France's HE has been widely explored (e.g. Castin, 2009; Jakobi & Rusconi, 2009; Malan, 2004; Musselin, 2009; Pilkington, 2012; Witte et al., 2008). This body of literature has emphasised several significant aspects of the BP in France, including the process of implementation and the consequences of the BP in France, the difficulties encountered during the implementation of the BP, and how BP reforms have served as a platform for the Europeanisation of HE in France.

Scholars have focused on several important transformations that happened in French HE with regard to the BP. Similar to other countries that are part of the EHEA, France has attempted to enhance its collaboration with others in HE, facilitating academic mobility (Malan, 2004) and promoting competitiveness and quality in HE (Castin, 2009; Musselin, 2009). Introducing three cycles of studies was another significant reform brought about by the BP. All these changes, along with the evolving neoliberal context, facilitated the development of the phenomenon of competitiveness among French higher education institutions (HEIs), as some recent studies explicate (e.g. Mai, 2022; Sánchez-Chaparro et al., 2020), as well as the rise of quality assurance pursuits (Benito & Romera, 2011; Sánchez-Chaparro et al., 2020). Batechko and Durdas (2020) argue that the French approach to evaluating the quality of HE already operates on multiple levels, providing university staff with the means to assess the advancement of the HE practice.

These transformations in the French HE, guided by the BP, have been accompanied by a range of challenges. One example of such challenges is related to the competitiveness aspect mentioned above as a correlation has developed between university autonomy and university rankings in France (Mai, 2022). Aust and Musselin (2014) highlight a significant impact of university rankings on the transformation of the French HE system, particularly in shaping the evaluation criteria for university performance, which revealed weaknesses in French HE. French universities' initial poor performance in rankings created the need for the reform of the HE system as many French HE institutions did not have the characteristics necessary for the representability in the ranking (i.e. having large comprehensive universities, publishing in English-speaking journals [Aust & Musselin, 2014; Highman, 2021]). Another challenge was in the implementation of the three-cycle study system which met resistance from universities which were used to doing things differently in accordance with the previously established conventions. For example, academics criticised the reform, emphasising its failure to adequately address the needs and demands of students and the labour market (Castin, 2009).

Such BP-induced structural reforms in French HE came to be associated with Europeanisation in and beyond HE in France. Some scholars mention that the BP should be analysed as a process of Europeanisation rather than only as a set of

HE reforms (Dakowska, 2019; Dobbins, 2017; Kushnir & Yazgan, 2023; Musselin, 2009; Pilkington, 2012; Sacilotto-Vasylenko, 2013). The mere fact of European Commission's involvement in governing the BP was a clue by Dakowska (2019) to argue for the need of such an analysis. According to her, the European Commission's influence is strengthened through the deployment of its experts, who act as policy brokers, working to promote a broader European agenda at the domestic levels of the EHEA signatory countries. This allows the EU's clientele to engage with domestic actors, including those in France, in order to advocate for European policies (Dakowska, 2019).

The overlapping gaps in prior relevant research were explained in Chapters 1 and 3. To remind, with regard to the French case, the literature presented above has focused on the state of affairs with respect to France's membership in the EHEA after 2020, France has not been analysed as a founding country of the EHEA along with the other three founders, and the link between France's membership in the EHEA and France's wider politics have not been scrutinised.

5.4 An Instrumental Role of France's Membership in the European Higher Education Area in Moderating the European Project

The analysis of the interviews and official communications from key EHEA stakeholders in France has demonstrated their perspectives on the role of HE in Europe post-2020, including the significance of France's membership in the EHEA for France, the insight this gives us about France's wider Europeanisation agenda and the evolving mission of the European project. The below discussion focuses specifically on what we have learned about France's stakeholders seeing France as one of key leaders of Europe in general as well as its HE in particular and seeing HE cooperation as a gateway to friendship in the European region, although it is not an easy achievement.

The data from this project echo the sentiment in the scholarship about France's leadership role in the European region (Krotz & Schild, 2013; Schmidt, 2020; Sutton, 2007) along with Germany (Degner & Leuffen, 2019). However, while Germany is considered to be a stronger leader overall (Aggestam & Hyde-Price, 2020), French Bologna stakeholders see France and Germany more as equal partners in the leading of Europe when it comes to leadership through education:

> We think that Europe works well when France and Germany work together for Europe. That's the type of situation where we regard ourselves as leaders, basically. Sometimes embarrassing actually... we regard ourselves as the leaders of Europe. That's basically what it is. Let's say one of the leaders of Europe.... (C3, representative of the Assembly of Directors of University Institutes of Technology (ADIUT))

Given this leadership role of France in Europe, it would not come as a surprise that France leads the way in terms of education developments, particularly in HE:

> ...our president, Emmanuel Macron, has made everything in order for higher education in France to lead the way and to fit in the European system. He wants France to be an example for the higher education field in Europe, and so he has made everything for it to be true. (C4, representative of a national student organisation (FAGE))

The interviewee refers to the European Universities Initiative in the quote above that is an aspect of the European Education Area which has increasingly been interlinked with the EHEA developments (Wagenaar, 2022). Kempin (2021) acknowledges that the overarching strategic aim of the European Universities Initiative is cultural integration in Europe; however, this is presented again as a vision shared by the two key leaders of Europe, namely France and Germany. However, the interview above exemplifies the idea expressed by others implying a greater importance of France in this process. Regarding specifically the EHEA, France's leadership position in European HE was evident in its preparation for the EHEA 2020 ministerial conference hosted by Italy. As illustrated by an official communication of the French Ministry of Higher Education, Research and Innovation (2019), prior to the conference, France launched a national consultation on the prospects of the EHEA to which higher education establishments in France as well as the wider public were invited to respond.

A key reason for France to aim to develop European HE is because, evidently, France's Bologna stakeholders choose to see HE cooperation as a gateway to strengthening 'the attractiveness of the Europe zone' (The French Ministry of Higher Education, Research and Innovation, 2020) and cross-country friendships in the European region:

> ...the attack [of Russia] on Ukraine shows... that if we don't act as a continent, we just are going to lose millions of our citizens... Some people, as I said, the extreme right or the extreme left will criticise Europe and say that we would be better without. But I mean those attract a very small amount of the vote... But I'd say that every one is absolutely convinced that education, and a European education is our way forward. I'm sure there's no question about that. (C3, representative of the Assembly of Directors of University Institutes of Technology (ADIUT))

According to the rational-choice strand of neo-institutionalism, such as choice to view HE as such is a rational decision. The unifying role of HE in Europe in the framework of the EHEA has also started pointing to a greater appreciation by the French Bologna stakeholders of the links between an HE community and a peaceful wider community:

> ...the present events in Ukraine [invasion by Russia] show in retrospect that we were right to start working on European community. And at least there's a European community of higher education... And if we are not able to have a perfect democracy everywhere, at least we are able to share. (C3, representative of the Assembly of Directors of University Institutes of Technology (ADIUT))

This implies that the old peace-building sentiment that prompted the development of the European project (Polyakova, 2016) has started gaining momentum again. However, it is:

> ...challenging to have team 'EHEA'. Of course, you've got two areas in one, EU and non-EU, and the western side and the eastern side... it's a strategy to be in the EHEA as a member. (C2, French expert in the Bologna Process)

Internal and external instabilities from the Euro crisis of 2010s through to Brexit and the COVID-19 pandemic (Ferrara & Kriesi, 2022; Schimmelfennig, 2021) have challenged European integration. These crises have brought the discussions about European disintegration to the forefront (Patberg, 2021). Such discussions may even question whether the EHEA is immune to similar disintegration processes. For example, recent populist gains in France (Chabal & Behrent, 2024) may also, arguably, become reflected in the French cooperation strategy with European partners in the framework of the EHEA in the future. Nonetheless, as the EHEA is committed to such European values as democracy and the rule of law, it should be able to serve as a platform to bring these values and ideas back on track. This is illustrated in the following quote:

> The only way for us, as a country, as an economic force, but also as a group of citizens is to have a fully functional Europe, and therefore a fully functional EHEA. (C3, representative of the Assembly of Directors of University Institutes of Technology (ADIUT))

Undoubtedly, inclusive education provision is a core element of innovation (The French Ministry of Higher Education, Research and Innovation, 2022) and democracy (Bergan, 2022). A similar position of the Bologna stakeholders in France can be illustrated by the quote from the same representative of the ADIUT:

> ...we need to provide more education, more democracy. (C3)

Some EU countries have recently experienced an illiberal turn which signals of a democratic decline which influences not just the EU but also a wider Europe. This suggests a value change in countries such as Hungary, and this may, arguably, cause an ideational clash with other members of the EHEA in relation to such issues as academic freedom. The expelling of the Central European University from Budapest in 2018 and its move to Austria (Enyedi et al., 2019) is a telling example of this.

EHEA's dedication to institutional autonomy and academic freedom, and student and staff mobility has become more important in the current political climate (Gallagher, 2018). This potential of the EHEA for shaping the wider politics is what Gallagher (2018) sees as HE's civic and social role.

5.5 Conclusion

This chapter has shed light on French EHEA stakeholders' perspectives on the role of HE in Europe, particularly in the current context post-Brexit and post-COVID, yet with still an ongoing invasion of Ukraine. The data have demonstrated that France BP stakeholders see France as one of key leaders of Europe in general as well as its HE in particular, and they also see HE cooperation as a gateway to friendship in the European region, albeit it is not an easy task to achieve. The data above point to important insights into underlying political elements of the EHEA. The analysis of the data suggests that there is an association between EHEA membership and wider politics, which is the idea furthered in the next data chapters.

References

Aggestam, L., & Hyde-Price, A. (2020). Learning to lead? Germany and the leadership paradox in EU foreign policy. *German Politics, 29*(1), 8–24. https://doi.org/10.1080/09644008.2019.1601177

Altiparmakis, A., Bojar, A., Brouard, S., Foucault, M., Kriesi, H., & Nadeau, R. (2021). Pandemic politics: Policy evaluations of government responses to COVID-19. *West European Politics, 44*(5–6), 1159–1179. https://doi.org/10.1080/01402382.2021.1930754

Aust, J., & Musselin, C. (2014, July). The reconfiguration of the French university landscape as an indirect consequence of the Shangay rankings, or how rankings indirectly affect the design of higher education systems. In Paper presented at *European Group of Organisational Studies (EGOS) Colloquium*, Rotterdam, NL.

Bajos, N., Spire, A., & Silberzan, L., & EPICOV Study Group. (2022). The social specificities of hostility toward vaccination against Covid-19 in France. *PLoS One, 17*(1). https://doi.org/10.1371/journal.pone.0262192

Batechko, N., & Durdas, A. (2020). The French model for assessing the quality of higher education: Current trends. *Continuing Professional Education: Theory and Practice, 1*, 93–98. http://doi.org/10.28925/1609-8595.2020.1.14

BBC. (2024, August 27). Macron rules out leftist PM as crisis continues. https://www.bbc.co.uk/news/articles/cevj87eypewo. Accessed on August 27, 2024.

Benito, M., & Romera, R. (2011). Improving quality assessment of composite indicators in university rankings: A case study of French and German universities of excellence. *Scientometrics*, *89*(1), 153–176. https://doi.org/10.1007/s11192-011-0419-5

Bergan, S. (2022). Education for democracy: Balancing intellectual rigor and political action. In M. Klemencic (Ed.), *From actors to reforms in European higher education: A Festschrift for Pavel Zgaga* (pp. 239–251). Springer International Publishing. https://doi.org/10.1007/978-3-031-09400-2_17

Bourdin, S., & Torre, A. (2023). Geography of contestation: A study on the Yellow Vest movement and the rise of populism in France. *Journal of Regional Science*, *63*(1), 214–235. https://doi.org/10.1111/jors.12620

Bouza García, L., & Oleart, Á. (2022). Make Europe great again: The politicising pro-European narrative of Emmanuel Macron in France. In T. Haapala & A. Oleart (Eds.), *Tracing the politicisation of the EU: The future of Europe debates before and after the 2019 elections* (pp. 271–293). https://doi.org/10.1007/978-3-030-82700-7

Brouard, S., Vasilopoulos, P., & Becher, M. (2020). Sociodemographic and psychological correlates of compliance with the COVID-19 public health measures in France. *Canadian Journal of Political Science [Revue Canadienne de Science Politique]*, *53*(2), 253–258. https://doi.org/10.1017/S0008423920000335

Capati, A. (2024). The COVID-19 pandemic and institutional change in the EU's financial assistance regime: The governance of the recovery and resilience facility (RRF). *Journal of European Integration*, *46*(3), 341–363. https://doi.org/10.1080/07036337.2023.2294722

Carpiano, R. M., Callaghan, T., DiResta, R., Brewer, N. T., Clinton, C., Galvani, A. P., & Hotez, P. J. (2023). Confronting the evolution and expansion of anti-vaccine activism in the USA in the COVID-19 era. *The Lancet*, *401*, 967–970. https://doi.org/10.1016/S0140-6736(23)00136-8

Castin, L. (2009). The implementation of the Bologna Process in France: Existing paradoxes and remaining obstacles. In C. F. Bonser (Ed.), *Adapting universities to the global society: A transatlantic perspective* (pp. 83–93). Lit Verlag.

Chabal, E., & Behrent, M. C. (2024). The deluge: France's 2024 legislative elections. *Modern & Contemporary France*, *32*(3), 329–337. https://doi.org/10.1080/09639489.2024.2381787

Clegg, D. (2022). A more liberal France, a more social Europe? Macron, two-level reformism and the COVID-19 crisis. *Comparative European Politics*, *20*(2), 184–200. https://doi.org/10.1057/s41295-022-00279-4

Dakowska, D. (2019). Decentring European higher education governance: The construction of expertise in the Bologna Process. In M. Bevir & R. Philips (Eds.), *Decentring European governance* (pp. 82–101). Routledge. https://doi.org/10.4324/9781351209557

Degner, H., & Leuffen, D. (2019). Franco-German cooperation and the rescuing of the Eurozone. *European Union Politics*, *20*(1), 89–108. https://doi.org/10.1177/1465116518811076

Dobbins, M. (2017). Convergent or divergent Europeanisation? An analysis of higher education governance reforms in France and Italy. *International Review of Administrative Sciences*, *83*(1), 177–199. https://doi.org/10.1177/0020852315580498

Douenne, T., & Fabre, A. (2020). French attitudes on climate change, carbon taxation and other climate policies. *Ecological Economics*, *169*. https://doi.org/10.1016/j.ecolecon.2019.106496

Duyvendak, J. W. (2019). *The power of politics: New social movements in France*. Routledge.
Enyedi, Z., Kovács, J. M., & Trencsényi, B. (2019). The Central European University in the trenches. In J. M. Kovacs & B. BTrencsenyi (Eds.), *Brave new Hungary: Mapping the system of national cooperation* (pp. 243–266). Lexington Books.
Ferrara, F. M., & Kriesi, H. (2022). Crisis pressures and European integration. *Journal of European Public Policy*, *29*(9), 1351–1373. https://doi.org/10.1080/13501763.2021.1966079
Gagneux-Brunon, A., Botelho-Nevers, E., Bonneton, M., Peretti-Watel, P., Verger, P., Launay, O., & Ward, J. K. (2022). Public opinion on a mandatory COVID-19 vaccination policy in France: A cross-sectional survey. *Clinical Microbiology and Infection*, *28*(3), 433–439. https://doi.org/10.1016/j.cmi.2021.10.016
Gallagher, T. (2018). Promoting the civic and democratic role of higher education: The next challenge for the EHEA? In A. Curaj, L. Deca, & R. Pricopie (Eds.), *European Higher Education Area: The impact of past and future policies* (pp. 335–344). Springer Nature. https://doi.org/10.1007/978-3-319-77407-7
Giurlando, P. (2021). Emmanuel Macron's challenge: Ensuring proximate parity with Germany. *Modern and Contemporary France*, *29*(1), 57–74. https://doi.org/10.1080/09639489.2020.1849080
Highman, L. (2021). Emerging from the mist: French universities and global rankings. *International Higher Education*, *105*, 37–38.
Jakobi, A. P., & Rusconi, A. (2009). Lifelong learning in the Bologna process: European developments in higher education. *Compare*, *39*(1), 51–65. https://doi.org/10.1080/03057920801936977
Jetten, J., Mols, F., & Selvanathan, H. P. (2020). How economic inequality fuels the rise and persistence of the Yellow Vest movement. *International Review of Social Psychology*, *33*(1), 1–12. https://doi.org/10.5334/irsp.356
Kempin, R. (2021). *France's foreign and security policy under president Macron: The consequences for Franco-German cooperation*. SWP Research Paper. https://doi.org/10.18449/2021RP04
Krotz, U., & Schild, J. (2013). *Shaping Europe: France, Germany, and embedded bilateralism from the Elysée treaty to twenty-first century politics*. Oxford University Press.
Krotz, U., & Schramm, L. (2022). Embedded bilateralism, integration theory, and European crisis politics: France, Germany, and the birth of the EU corona recovery fund. *JCMS: Journal of Common Market Studies*, *60*(3), 526–544. https://doi.org/10.1111/jcms.13251
Kushnir, I. (2023). 'It is more than just education. It's also a peace policy': (Re)imagining the mission of the European Higher Education Area in the context of the Russian invasion of Ukraine. *European Educational Research Journal*, 1–16. https://doi.org/10.1177/14749041231200927
Kushnir, I., Kilkey, M., & Strumia, F. (2020). EU integration in the (post)-migrant-crisis context: Learning new integration modes? *European Review*, *28*(2), 306–324. https://doi.org/10.1017/S1062798719000425
Kushnir, I., & Yazgan, N. (2023). The politics of higher education: The European Higher Education Area through the eyes of its stakeholders in France and Italy. *Humanities and Social Sciences Communications*, *10*(1), 1–11. https://doi.org/10.1057/s41599-023-02300-x

Ladrech, R. (1994). Europeanisation of domestic politics and institutions: The case of France. *Journal of Common Market Studies*, *32*(1), 69–88. https://doi.org/10.1111/j.1468-5965.1994.tb00485.x

Mai, A. N. (2022). The effect of autonomy on university rankings in Germany, France and China. *Higher Education for the Future*, *9*(1), 75–92. https://doi.org/10.1177/23476311211046178

Major, C. (2021). A committed but challenging ally: France's NATO policy. In R. Kempin (Ed.), *France's foreign and security policy under president Macron: The consequences for Franco–German cooperation*. SWP Research Paper. https://doi.org/10.18449/2021RP04

Malan, T. (2004). Implementing the Bologna Process in France. *European Journal of Education*, *39*(3), 289–297. https://doi.org/10.1111/j.1465-3435.2004.00184.x

Musselin, C. (2009). *The side effects of the Bologna Process on national institutional settings: The case of France*. Springer Netherlands. https://doi.org/10.1007/978-1-4020-9505-4_8

Ostermann, F., & Stahl, B. (2022). Theorizing populist radical-right foreign policy: Ideology and party positioning in France and Germany. *Foreign Policy Analysis*, *18*(3). https://doi.org/10.1093/fpa/orac006

Patberg, M. (2021). The democratic ambivalence of EU disintegration: A mapping of costs and benefits. *Swiss Political Science Review*, *27*(3), 601–618. https://doi.org/10.1111/spsr.12455

Pilkington, M. (2012). The French evolution: France and the Europeanisation of higher education. *Journal of Higher Education Policy and Management*, *34*(1), 39–50. https://doi.org/10.1080/1360080X.2012.642330

Polyakova, A. (2016). The great European unravelling? *World Policy Journal*, *33*(4), 68–72. https://doi.org/10.1215/07402775-3813051

Sacilotto-Vasylenko, M. (2013). Bologna process and initial teacher education reform in France. In M. Akiba (Ed.), *Teacher reforms around the world: Implementations and outcomes* (pp. 3–24). Emerald Publishing Limited. https://doi.org/10.1108/S1479-3679(2013)0000019006

Sánchez-Chaparro, T., Gómez-Frías, V., & González-Benito, Ó. (2020). Competitive implications of quality assurance processes in higher education. The case of higher education in engineering in France. *Economic research-Ekonomska istraživanja*, *33*(1), 2825–2843. https://doi.org/10.1080/1331677X.2019.1697329

Schild, J. (2013). Leadership in hard times: Germany, France, and the management of the Eurozone crisis. *German Politics and Society*, *31*(1), 24–47. https://doi.org/10.3167/gps.2013.310103

Schimmelfennig, F. (2021). Rebordering Europe: External boundaries and integration in the European Union. *Journal of European Public Policy*, *28*(3), 311–330. https://doi.org/10.1080/13501763.2021.1881589

Schmidt, V. A. (2020). Trapped by their ideas: French élites' discourses of European integration and globalisation. In E. Grossman (Ed.), *France and the European Union* (pp. 1–18). Routledge. https://doi.org/10.4324/9781003061007

Steible, B. (2022). Emmanuel Macron: The return of France as a driving force for European integration? In D. R. Ramiro Troitiño, R. Martín de la Guardia, & G. A. Pérez Sánchez (Eds.), *The European Union and its political leaders: Understanding the integration process* (pp. 279–294). Springer International Publishing.

Sutton, M. (2007). *France and the construction of Europe, 1944-2007*. Berghahn Books. https://doi.org/10.3167/9781845453930

The French Ministry of Higher Education, Research and Innovation. (2019). National consultation on the future of Europe and Higher Education. https://www.enseignementsup-recherche.gouv.fr/fr/consultation-nationale-sur-le-futur-de-l-europe-et-de-l-enseignement-superieur-49136. Accessed on September 4, 2024.

The French Ministry of Higher Education, Research and Innovation. (2020). E.H.E.A.: Policy instruments. https://www.enseignementsup-recherche.gouv.fr/fr/eees-les-instruments-de-la-politique-46489. Accessed on September 4, 2024.

The French Ministry of Higher Education, Research and Innovation. (2022). PFUE: Higher education, research and innovation program. https://www.enseignementsup-recherche.gouv.fr/fr/pfue-programme-de-l-enseignement-superieur-de-la-recherche-et-de-l-innovation-83243. Accessed on September 4, 2024.

Vail, M. I., Watson, S., & Driscoll, D. (2023). Representation and displacement: Labor disembedding and contested neoliberalism in France. *Comparative Politics, 55*(3), 377–400.

Vertier, P., Viskanic, M., & Gamalerio, M. (2023). Dismantling the "Jungle": Migrant relocation and extreme voting in France. *Political Science Research and Methods, 11*(1), 129–143. https://doi.org/10.1017/psrm.2022.26

Wagenaar, R. (2022). The myth of power: Governing reform in the Bologna Process of higher education. In M. Klemencic (Ed.), *From actors to reforms in European higher education: A Festschrift for Pavel Zgaga* (pp. 45–63). Springer International Publishing. https://doi.org/10.1007/978-3-031-09400-2_17

Webber, D. (Ed.) (2005). *The Franco–German relationship in the EU*. Routledge. https://doi.org/10.4324/9780203983355

Witte, J., Van der Wende, M., & Huisman, J. (2008). Blurring boundaries: How the Bologna process changes the relationship between university and non-university higher education in Germany, the Netherlands and France. *Studies in Higher Education, 33*(3), 217–231. https://doi.org/10.1080/03075070802049129

Chapter 6

Italy's Membership in the European Higher Education Area: Coordinating Cooperation in Higher Education While Attempting to Stay Apolitical

Authored by Iryna Kushnir and Nuve Yazgan

Abstract

This chapter analyses the politics of Italian Bologna stakeholders' membership in the European Higher Education Area (EHEA) and the significance of this for the European region in the early 2020s. Drawing on neo-institutionalism and relying on seven in-depth interviews with key Italian Bologna stakeholders and their official communications, as well as some international-level EHEA communications, the chapter demonstrates a leading position of Italy in the development of the higher education vision and politics in the EHEA since the Rome ministerial conference in 2020. However, Italy's trialling of whether it is possible to remain apolitical in their work in the EHEA, which is by default a politically charged behaviour, has been explicitly focused on the Europeanisation particularly of relevant higher education initiatives rather than of the European region.

Keywords: Italy; Bologna Process; European Higher Education Area; Europe; policy; politics

6.1 Introduction

This chapter focuses on Italy, which is the third of the four elements of the collective case study of the perspectives of the founders of the European Higher Education Area (EHEA) regarding the role of European cooperation in higher education (HE), represented by the EHEA, in the evolving mission of the European project in the early 2020s.

The neo-institutionalist approach which frames the analysis in this book was explained in Chapter 2. All the methodological decisions that underpin the project reported in this book were presented in the introductory chapter, but it is important to remind here that the Italian case rests on a thematic analysis of seven in-depth semi-structured elite interviews with an opportunistic/snowball sample of key Bologna stakeholders in Italy and 10 of their official communications.[1] The interviewees include a couple of key HE actors in Italy who wished to keep their organisational affiliation unrevealed, a former vice-chair of the Bologna Follow-up Group in Italy as well as representatives from the Italian quality assurance agency (ANVUR), the national Union of University Students (UDU) and the Conference of Italian University Rectors (CRUI).

This chapter starts with explaining recent developments in Italian politics which is essential contextual information for our analysis below. This is then followed by a review of literature on EHEA's Bologna Process (BP) in Italy and presenting key findings about Italian EHEA stakeholders' perspectives on the role of HE in Europe after 2020.

The chapter demonstrates that Italian EHEA-related stakeholders, despite taking a coordinating role in the EHEA, have been trialing ways of staying apolitical before succumbing to the unavoidable connection between politics and HE. This attitude to politics may, arguably, be rooted predominantly in the assumed conflict between EHEA's inherent link to Europeanisation (Kushnir & Yazgan, 2023) and Italy's growing Euroscepticism, coupled with a commitment to maintaining security in the region (Albertazzi & Zulianello, 2021; Conti et al., 2020; D'Alimonte, 2019; Pasquinucci, 2022).

6.2 Recent Developments in Italian Politics

This section maps the field of prior research on the Italian political landscape. According to historical neo-institutionalism (Peters, 2019), it is an essential context for the analysis of Italy's views on the role of the EHEA in the European project. This context is also key to understand the rationalisation – rational decision-making – process of the Italian Bologna stakeholders. The analysis of it later in this chapter will be guided by the rational-choice strand of neo-institutionalism.

Right wing parties have exerted a significant influence over Italian politics over the past 25 years by emphasising immigration, law and order, Euroscepticism and tax reduction promises. This strategy was greatly shaped by the Forza Italia (FI) and its leader Berlusconi, who entered politics in 1994 (Albertazzi et al., 2021). Italy's traditional two-party system has collapsed, with the 2013 elections leading

---

[1]The dataset with interview transcripts, generated and analysed during the research project that informs this book, is available in the Research Data Archive of Nottingham Trent University, at https://doi.org/10.17631/RD-2022-0001-DDOC.

to the instability of the coalition governments in the coming years (Chiaramonte & Emanuele, 2013). This was due to Prime Minister Berlusconi who encountered a series of scandals and legal proceedings related to his personal affairs and business dealings. The 2013 elections led two centre-right and centre-left parties, the party Il Popolo della Libertà (PdL) and the democratic party Partito Democraticoarty (PD), to lose power (Chiaramonte & Emanuele, 2013). The 2013 electoral victory of the then populist Five Star Movement (M5s) party delegitimised the traditional ruling political class. After Berlusconi's conviction in 2013, he was prevented from holding public office until 2019, which prevented him from running as a candidate in the 2018 parliamentary elections or aspiring to the position of Prime Minister (Donà, 2022). It is worth noting the that the M5s party has undergone a change in how it is perceived by the public on the political spectrum with it shaping itself as being beyond the left-right duality (Giannetti et al., 2024).

The rise of populism in Italy has been a hot topic in a recent growing body of relevant literature (Albertazzi & Zulianello, 2021; Conti et al., 2020; D'Alimonte, 2019; Di Matteo & Mariotti, 2021; Pasquinucci, 2022; Zulianello, 2022). Italian modern populism holds its roots in the 1990s and the devolution of the two-party system (D'Alimonte, 2019). A few recent studies (Albertazzi & Zulianello, 2021; D'Alimonte, 2019; Di Matteo & Mariotti, 2021; Zulianello, 2022) have demonstrated that recent populist gains in Italy can be explained taking into account the links with the economic and related institutional problems in Italy as well as the issues related to migration into the European region which have had an impact on Italy as well. In particular, these scholars highlight the consolidation of the League which is the right-wing political party as well as the M5s, with its complex identity endorsing populism and claiming to be beyond the left-right division (Albertazzi & Zulianello, 2021; Conti et al., 2020). Albertazzi and Zulianello (2021) investigate regional cleavages in this populist consolidation by contrasting the League with the M5s which happen to have divergent agendas, albeit both populist. According to them, the League has gained its success through cultural cleavages, while the M5s has gained its popularity through focusing on economy and institutions, and thus, on a Eurosceptic electoral campaign. The 2018 elections in Italy resulted in a historic victory of the populist forces (D'Alimonte, 2019). An incrementally increasing gap between the Italian elites and the rest of the population has brought about the popularity of the League and M5s as they have been promising a radical change for the country (D'Alimonte, 2019). Similar trends have gained traction in other countries across the European Union (EU) (Pasquinucci, 2022).

With the 2018 elections, the M5s and the League emerged victorious and they joined forces to establish the Conte I government, which held power from June 2018 to September 2019 (Donà, 2022). However, a year later, the Conte I government was replaced by a coalition involving the M5s, the Democratic Party and other smaller left-wing parties, resulting in the formation of the Conte II government, which governed between September 2019 and February 2021. Due to the instability of the coalition, the President of the Republic made the decision to invite Mario Draghi, the former President of the European Central Bank, to form a new government in February 2021 (Donà, 2022). The Italian elections of 2022 were called following Mario Draghi's resignation. Arguably, a combination of those developments and the 2022 elections, in particular, have led to the normalisation of the populist right in Italy (Zulianello, 2022).

Another populist right-wing party, FdI (Brothers of Italy) won the 2022 elections leading Giorgia Meloni to become the first female Prime Minister of the country. Her party promotes conservative values, national identity, and Euroscepticism. It advocates for stricter immigration policies, traditional family values, and economic nationalism (Donà, 2022). Meloni's triumph presents the culmination of a gradual process of normalising and integrating populist ideologies within Italian politics that commenced in the early 1990s (Zulianello, 2022). The composition of the latest government is historically significant as it consists of two populist parties who represent about 80% of the votes (Donà, 2022). Italy's national results of the 2024 European elections have shown that 'Prime Minister Giorgia Meloni's Fratelli d'Italia party has won European elections in Italy with a whopping 28% of votes. Analysts say she secured herself as kingmaker in the European Parliament' (Euronews, 2024). However, regional elections in Italy in 2024 have put Meloni's nearly pan-Italian support into questions. For instance, The Guardian (2024) reports that:

> The Italian prime minister, Giorgia Meloni, has suffered her first regional election setback since taking power after a leftwing candidate was elected president of Sardinia. Alessandra Todde, a politician with the Five Star Movement (M5S) who was backed by the Democratic party (PD), has become the island's first female president, narrowly beating Paolo Truzzu, the rightwing candidate chosen by Meloni.

The presentation of the M5s as a left-wing party is, of course, debatable but not entirely surprising, given the complexity of M5s shifting identity (Giannetti et al., 2024).

Italy's relations with the EU have also been affected by the migration flows shaping public attitudes towards the EU and its institutions. Italy has been one of the forefront countries on the immigration route of the people fleeing from countries such as Syria and Afghanistan following the war in Syria. After Greece, Italy has served as the country of first arrival for refugees who reach Europe via sea routes (Castelli-Gattinara, 2017). The influx of migrants combined with the authorities' weaknesses in managing the arrival of migrants has led to tensions with the EU. Additionally, it has sparked public controversies regarding the scale and financial implications of Italy's involvement in patrol operations (Castelli-Gattinara, 2017).

The migration crisis has served as a substitute for significant changes within the Italian party politics – in other words the right-wing populist surge (Geddes & Pettrachin, 2020). The migration issue was politicised by the political elite and the media (Caponio & Cappiali, 2018). Immigration has become a high-stake issue in Italian politics often appropriated by the populist movement (Dennison &

Geddes, 2022), resulting in a form of a politically saturated hostility (Barisione, 2020).

Apart from the issues discussed above, Italy has also been challenged by the Covid-19 pandemic and the Climate Change in the recent years. Scholars suggest a mismanagement of the pandemic during the first phases due to undertaking some rapid measures and a lack of coordination between political and scientific elites (Bull, 2021; Ruiu, 2020; Sanfelici, 2020). Overall, the crises have sparked a growing discussion regarding the future of the EU integration/disintegration (Hutter & Kriesi, 2020; Riddervold et al., 2021). Such developments have contributed to a high degree of Euroscepticism in Italy, especially by those populist far-right parties that have also used the European financial crisis as a matter of discussion as it also affected Italy (Conti et al., 2020). The economic and political challenges faced by the country, coupled with such issues as immigration and the perceived lack of equal treatment by the EU have contributed to Eurosceptic sentiments (Conti et al., 2020). For instance, both M5s and the League framed immigration issue to criticise the EU (Alonso-Muñoz & Casero-Ripollés, 2020). For the M5s, Italy was left alone in dealing with a migration flows, and they argue that European countries needed to fairly distribute the migrants. The League holds a considerably more rigid stance advocating for a complete ban on immigrants entering Italy and advocates for the establishment of a different Europe that prioritises security, traditional family values and Christianity (Alonso-Muñoz & Casero-Ripollés, 2020).

6.3 The Bologna Process in Italy

The adoption of the EHEA-related reforms in Italy has been examined by a range of scholars (Aittola et al., 2009; Ballarino & Perotti, 2012; Cammelli et al., 2011; Chies et al., 2019; Di Pietro, 2012; Guccio et al., 2016; Jakobi & Rusconi, 2009; Moscati, 2009; Ursin et al., 2008).

Being one of the founders of the BP, Italy was, of course, among the first few countries to start adopting the BP which has been a process with many successes along the way, as well as a range of challenges (e.g., Ballarino & Perotti, 2012; Cammelli et al., 2011; Di Pietro, 2012; Guccio et al., 2016; Moscati, 2009). The BP-related reforms in the Italian HE system have been the most significant reforms in the area of education in general ever accomplished in the country (Ballarino & Perotti, 2012) and there is a lot to celebrate regarding the achievements of the implementation process. In particular, the BP reforms have had a positive impact on university enrolment rates in Italy (Di Pietro, 2012), and teaching efficiency in Italian universities has improved significantly (Guccio et al., 2016).

The 1990s marked early efforts towards modernisation and the development of a focus on HE quality assurance in Italy. Early attempts proved to be ineffective due to a lack of transparency in university management structures and resistance from the academic community. In 1999, the *Comitato Nazionale la valutazione del sistema universitario* (CNVSU) was established to review university self-evaluation reports, and student participation was encouraged through the use of questionnaires to evaluate teaching activities. In 2010, a new national quality assurance body ANVUR (*Agenzia Nazionale di Valutazione del Sistema Universitario e della Ricerca*) was created. Significant aspects of this framework were influenced by the French and British quality assurance institutions (Dobbins et al., 2023). A significant change that took place was the introduction of an accreditation system. This change resulted in the establishment of a new organisational unit known as the Quality Assurance Committee (QAC), which now oversees quality assurance processes (Agasisti et al., 2019).

These reforms have taken place not without criticism. Critical voices have been sounding regarding the lack of improvements that the lifelong learning initiatives have brought about (Jakobi & Rusconi, 2009). Similarly, HE quality assurance practices in Italy have also faced criticism (Ursin et al., 2008), evidenced by questioning university student performance and reasons behind persistent social inequalities in graduation rates in spite of the Bologna reforms (Chies et al., 2019). There has been a well-known socio-economic division between the northern and southern regions in the country which have caused an imbalanced flow of students, with a significant number migrating to the northern regions for university studies. The areas that are economically disadvantaged tend to have lower rates of high school graduates transitioning to university, lower graduation rates and eventually a higher likelihood of students migrating in search of employment opportunities (Columbu et al., 2021). Santelli et al. (2022) who examine student mobility in the southern Campania region find that students are drawn to prestigious universities in the northern regions, particularly when they want to pursue a Master's degree.

In spite of the lack of official barriers to entry, Italy is falling behind most developed nations when it comes to the percentage of young people who have completed HE (Contini & Salza, 2020). Cappellari and Lucifora (2009) examined Italian secondary school graduates both before and after the Bologna reform on the degree structure. They found that the reform had a substantial positive effect on the likelihood of people pursuing HE, particularly among students who were considered 'marginal'. These marginal students, characterised by strong academic abilities but disadvantaged family backgrounds, experienced a more pronounced increase in college enrolment as a result of the reform (Cappellari & Lucifora, 2009). Moreover, school to work transition in Italy is slow despite the labour market in Italy has undergone recent reforms that aimed to enhance flexibility by reducing the costs associated with hiring and firing (Pastore, 2019).

More recent studies about the membership of Italy in the EHEA focus on how the Italian HE system has evolved during the BP. Specifically, Beine et al. (2020) examine the trade-off between HE quality and costs at Italian institutions and maintain that those institutions which charge more in fees ended up with fewer international students, and this has resulted in less income from tuition fees. Another aspect of HE in Italy that has gained momentum in relevant scholarship is an increasing role of Italian HE institutions in promoting sustainability and social change (Frondizi et al., 2019). Also, Italian universities' entrepreneurial role (Vesperi & Gagnidze, 2021) and HE digitalisation (Piromalli, 2023) have also been addressed. In addition, the role of Italy in contributing to shaping the politics of the EHEA is also important in understanding how the driving role of Italy as a founder of the EHEA has changed (Kushnir & Yazgan, 2023).

The literature reviewed above seems to suggest that Italian membership in the EHEA still has an important role in Italy. This is despite the challenges in the implementation of relevant reforms. The gaps in relevant prior research on EHEA's founders' role in the EHEA and the link between the EHEA and wider politics were explained in Chapters 1 and 3. It is worth reminding here briefly that what concerns the Italian case, the literature review above has shown that the state of affairs with respect to Italy's membership in the EHEA after 2020 has not been the focus of attention, Italy has not been scrutinised as a founder of the EHEA by other scholars, and the relationship between Italy's EHEA membership and wider politics remains an under-researched area.

6.4 A Coordinating Role of Italy's Membership in the European Higher Education Area and the Politics of Attempted Apoliticism

The analysis of the interviews and official communications from key Italian Bologna stakeholders has shed light on their vision of the role of HE in Europe in the early 2020s. The section presents key findings and discusses them in light of the theoretical and empirical literature outlined in Chapters 2 and 3. These key findings focus on Italian stakeholders contributing to driving the development of the EHEA as a forum for cooperation in HE in the European region which, yet, cannot be separated from the wider politics of Europe; and on Italy's conflicting attitudes towards the politics in European cooperation in the area of HE.

6.4.1 The EHEA as a Forum for Cooperation in Higher Education in the European Region Intertwined With the Wider Politics of Europe

The EHEA has been evolving as an international forum for cooperation in the area of HE, as well as a base for exchanging knowledge more broadly – through allowing the development of connections among the EHEA signatories and offering a platform for a dialogue within the European region as well as between it and other regions worldwide. Resultingly, a tight link has been developing between HE cooperation within the EHEA and the wider politics of the countries that are members of the EHEA:

> We developed a vision of an open and inclusive European Higher Education Area. It is a political issue to make the EHEA as more open and inclusive as possible. We believe that having contacts with other geographical systems, education systems... is very important to connect, to have exchanges, to exchange good practices and so on. And this is from a political point of view. (D7, a representative of the Conference of Italian University Rectors (CRUI))

The same interviewee adds that the political flavour of the EHEA has been work in progress, as it has been evolving:

> The European Higher Education Area was a cultural project... maybe not at the very beginning. (D7)

Since the establishment of the EHEA, it has been instrumental in coordinating HE cooperation in the European region and beyond, predominantly by converging HE structures and pursuing a common vision (Kushnir, 2020). While HE policies have been EHEA's focus at least until the 2020 Rome Conference, there has been an unquestionable link between these policies and wider EHEA's politics, as suggested by the literature review presented in Chapter 3. The EHEA has been developed with the help of on the Open Method of Coordination. While such a governance mode is a non-binding way of cooperation, the shared nature of decision-making in the EHEA has been a strategic choice of EHEA stakeholders, following the logic of the rational-choice strand of neo-institutionalism explained in Chapter 2. Such a shared nature of decision-making within the EHEA, and the EHEA's recently updated aim of becoming 'inclusive, innovative and interconnected' (Rome Ministerial Communique, 2020, p. 3) illustrates the discussion in Chapter 3 – when the aspiration of building friendship among the countries is mirrored in HE, but also when cooperation in the area of HE becomes used to support wider politics.

It is important to acknowledge that this wider politics may have various stakes on democracy and human rights promotion. There are cases when authoritarianism in HE and the wider society mutually feed each other, such as in Russia and Belarus (Nikolayenko, 2021; Terzyan, 2019) or Afghanistan (Akbari & True, 2022). There are also more positive examples of HE being used for economic growth (Nyangau, 2014) or inter-county friendship promotion through Europeanisation (Huisman & Van Der Wende, 2004).

The politics specifically of the EU and the EHEA still seem to be intertwined even though the EHEA evidently transcends the borders of the EU:

> Of course, here the things that happen at the EU level are a bit overlapping with what happens at the EHEA level. (D2, key HE actor in Italy)

As explained in Chapter 3, HE became EU's instrument for Europeanisation a long time ago. To remind, the European Commission viewed HE as a tool to help develop a European single market, the idea of the European citizen (Keating, 2009) and European identity (Grek, 2008). The 1991 Memorandum on Higher Education demonstrated that HE was part of the European Commission's 'agenda of economic and social coherence' (Huisman & Van Der Wende, 2004, p. 350). These strategies were further embodied in the facilitation of the so-called 'European dimension' in the consolidated European HE space and searching for more cooperation opportunities which eventually brought about the start of the work on the EHEA (Robertson et al., 2016). Arguably, the expansion of the EHEA beyond EU's borders in the effort to build wider friendships in the European region and beyond (Kushnir, 2016). This was coupled by recent increasing gains of Euroscepticism within the EU (Vasilopoulou & Talving, 2024) which has inspired EU policy-makers to create the European Education Area. Its creation in 2017 has signified retracting to the idea of an education space specifically for the EU (Kushnir, 2021, 2022), while reserving the EHEA for the cooperation both within the EU as well as between the EU and nearby regions.

6.4.2 Paradoxes in Italy's Driving the EHEA: Its Understanding of Politics in HE Cooperation While Trying to Stay Apolitical

Having discussed the interconnectedness of the EHEA and European politics, which is evidently recognised by Italian Bologna stakeholders, it is now timely to draw attention to the paradoxically conflicting attitudes of Italian BP stakeholders in certain highly politically charged situations related to HE cooperation in the framework of the EHEA. The politics of attempted apoliticism on behalf of Italy in HE cooperation in the EHEA can be illustrated by the cases of responding to the repressions of students in Belarus who stood up to political injustice as well as to the Russian invasion of Ukraine.

Regarding Belarus, relevant scholarship is strikingly scarce, which may be a consequence of the censorship and surveillance prevalent in the country. During the presidency of Lukashenko since 1994, Belarus has been advancing its autocratic structures, whereby the President has had supreme decision-making powers, suppressing opposition voices through controlling the public space (Terzyan, 2019). This politics was also reflected in the relatively recent protests, joined by students, which was a reaction to the falsified 2020 election results in Belarus (Nikolayenko, 2023). The protests led to student arrests and expulsions from Belarusian universities. At least 466 students were detained and at least 153 students were expelled from their universities at the time (Amnesty International, 2021).

The data from the project reported in this book add an important aspect to the above limited scholarly debate. This aspect focuses on the accession and tolerating of Belarus as a member of the EHEA as seen by Italian Bologna stakeholders. First of all, the issues in Belarus HE, stemming for the above discussion of Belarus' wider politics, did cause precautions on the part of many EHEA members, particularly Italy. However, Belarus' accession into the EHEA was seen by Italy as a way to support members of the HE community in Belarus:

> Belarus is considered by some in the EHEA as – how to say – a not legitimate member. And I can see from working with them that unfortunately they had non-legitimate things going on before the invasion of Ukraine. And Belarus has the support of the Russian Federation... But I see that they were not any worse than Azerbaijan or some other countries... So before the invasion I did my best to support Belarus to help them. (D6, former vice-chair of the Bologna Follow-up Group in Italy)

However, the cooperation with Belarus has complicated reaching decisions particularly regarding EHEA's ambitions to promote academic freedom, university autonomy, etc.:

> We have seen that there were some problems, for example, in the case of Belarus and other countries. In principle, we agree, but when we have to decide a common action on general themes, then it is difficult. (D1, key HE actor in Italy)

While the condemnation of Belarus' politics is evident in the above quotes regarding Belarus' membership in the EHEA in general, responding to student repressions in Belarus during and after the 2020 presidential elections was less of a unanimous act among the Italian Bologna stakeholders, demonstrating that the Ministry of Education, Universities and Research in Italy was holding back:

> I'm working on fundamental values, and they [Italian ministry] were among those that haven't signed either the official statement condemning Belarussian repression during the Rome 2020 conference.... (D2, key HE actor in Italy)

Apparently, this Italian Ministry was considering similar abstinence during EHEA's preparation of the *Statement by members and consultative members of the Bologna Follow-up Group on consequences of the Russian invasion of Ukraine* (EHEA, 2022), which it eventually did sign and which was about suspending Russia and Belarus from the EHEA:

> We, therefore, ask the Bologna Follow Up Group (BFUG) to suspend the Russian Federation's rights of participation in all structures and activities of the EHEA, including the BFUG, working groups, task forces, peer learning groups and similar structures. We ask the BFUG to extend the same measures to Belarus. (EHEA, 2022, p. 1)

Motivations behind considering abstaining from signing the Statement above on the part of Italy was explained by a key HE actor in Italy:

> Basically, what they [Italian ministry] said is that they didn't want to [sign the letter to suspend Russia and Belarus]... They wanted the European Higher Education and the Bologna Process to not be involved with respect to political matters. So, to keep them separate. Now, it's very difficult that this is the position that can be taken, because the Russian Rectors' Conference has said yes, we support the war. So, also that makes it difficult to have this kind of position... It can also be that in general, there are countries that are less harsh towards Russia. Italy has historically been one of them. It might also be that they want to

do only the necessary and not the surplus. At the same time, I don't know whether this is the position because Italy's had struggles in many measures. So, it might be that there are other motivations or they will eventually sign. (D2)

However, the consideration not to respond would in itself be politically charged:

> ...there is a very high interest [in the Italian ministry] to keep these issues [response to the war] technical and not political, which is actually a political question. (D4, key higher education actor in Italy)

Nevertheless, the EHEA was able to take a unified action against Russia and Belarus for their cooperation in launching the invasion of Ukraine. This also included the voice from Italy which was paramount to stay in tune with the values that Italy had reaffirmed during the EHEA Conference in Rome in 2020, such as the freedom of speech, democracy, etc. (Rome Ministerial Communique, 2020). This demonstrates EHEA's wider objectives in addition to specifically HE policies by acting as a forum for uniting countries under common values. In spite of the issues that the European region has been facing, linked to populist gains, the EHEA has emerged as a major platform to foster a shared vision and commitment to democratic values:

> ...what is happening in Ukraine, means that also, being part of the Bologna is going to be, let's say, a commitment, a bigger commitment than it has been so far. (D2, key higher education actor in Italy)

On April 22, 2022, EHEA members, including Italy, issued the Statement in which the EHEA as an institution stated that the Russian aggression against Ukraine:

> ...disregards the values and goals of the EHEA and fundamentally violates all the obligations and commitments Russia has undertaken since it joined the EHEA in 2003. It has also undermined the trust that is fundamental to European higher education cooperation. For Russia to regain the trust of other EHEA members will be a long and difficult process. (EHEA, 2022, p. 1)

6.5 Conclusion

Chapter 6 has placed Italy at the centre of attention, which is the third of the four elements of the collective case study of the EHEA's founders' perspectives about the role of European cooperation in HE, represented by the EHEA initiatives, in our understanding of the evolving mission of the European project in the early 2020s. This chapter explained recent developments in

Italian politics as an essential contextual information for our analysis, followed by a review of literature on the BP in Italy and presenting key findings. The data have demonstrated that Italian stakeholders have been contributing to driving the development of the EHEA as a forum for cooperation in HE in the European region which, importantly, cannot be separated from the European wider politics, despite Italy's conflicting attitudes towards the politics of HE cooperation.

References

Agasisti, T., Barbato, G., Dal Molin, M., & Turri, M. (2019). Internal quality assurance in universities: Does NPM matter? *Studies in Higher Education*, *44*(6), 960–977.

Aittola, H., Kiviniemi, U., Honkimäki, S., Muhonen, R., Huusko, M., & Ursin, J. (2009). The Bologna process and internationalisation–consequences for Italian academic life. *Higher Education in Europe*, *34*(3–4), 303–312. https://doi.org/10.1080/03797720903355521

Akbari, F., & True, J. (2022). One year on from the Taliban takeover of Afghanistan: Re-instituting gender apartheid. *Australian Journal of International Affairs*, *76*(6), 624–633. https://doi.org/10.1080/10357718.2022.2107172

Albertazzi, D., Bonansinga, D., & Zulianello, M. (2021). The right-wing alliance at the time of the Covid-19 pandemic: All change? *Contemporary Italian Politics*, *13*(2), 181–195.

Albertazzi, D., & Zulianello, M. (2021). Populist electoral competition in Italy: The impact of sub-national contextual factors. *Contemporary Italian Politics*, *13*(1), 4–30. https://doi.org/10.1080/23248823.2020.1871186

Alonso-Muñoz, L., & Casero-Ripollés, A. (2020). Populism against Europe in social media: The eurosceptic discourse on Twitter in Spain, Italy, France, and United Kingdom during the campaign of the 2019 European Parliament election. *Frontiers in communication*, *5*, 54.

Amnesty International. (2021, May 24). Belarus university students expelled from universities and imprisoned for peaceful protest. https://www.amnesty.org/en/latest/press-release/2021/05/belarus-university-students-expelled-from-universities-and-imprisoned-for-peaceful-protest/. Accessed on August 26, 2024.

Ballarino, G., & Perotti, L. (2012). The Bologna Process in Italy. *European Journal of Education*, *47*(3), 348–363. https://doi.org/10.1111/j.1465-3435.2012.01530.x

Barisione, M. (2020). When ethnic prejudice is political: An experiment in beliefs and hostility toward immigrant out-groups in Italy. *Italian Political Science Review [Rivista Italiana di Scienza Politica]*, *50*(2), 213–234.

Beine, M., Delogu, M., & Ragot, L. (2020). The role of fees in foreign education: Evidence from Italy. *Journal of Economic Geography*, *20*(2), 571–600. https://doi.org/10.1093/jeg/lby044

Bull, M. (2021). The Italian government response to Covid-19 and the making of a prime minister. *Contemporary Italian Politics*, *13*(2), 149–165.

Cammelli, A., Antonelli, G., Francia, A. D., Gasperoni, G., & Sgarzi, M. (2011). Mixed outcomes of the Bologna Process in Italy. In H. Schomburg & U. Teichler (Eds.), *Employability and mobility of bachelor graduates in Europe: Key results of the Bologna Process* (pp. 143–170). SensePublishers. https://doi.org/10.1007/978-94-6091-570-3_7

Caponio, T., & Cappiali, T. M. (2018). Italian migration policies in times of crisis: The policy gap reconsidered. *South European Society and Politics, 23*(1), 115–132.

Cappellari, L., & Lucifora, C. (2009). The "Bologna Process" and college enrollment decisions. *Labour Economics, 16*(6), 638–647.

Castelli-Gattinara, P. (2017). The 'refugee crisis' in Italy as a crisis of legitimacy. *Contemporary Italian Politics, 9*(3), 318–331.

Chiaramonte, A., & Emanuele, V. (2013). Volatile and tripolar: The new Italian party system. In L. De Sio, V. Emanuele, N. Maggini, & A. Paparo (Eds.), *The Italian general election of 2013: A dangerous stalemate?* (pp. 63–68). CISE.

Chies, L., Graziosi, G., & Pauli, F. (2019). The impact of the Bologna Process on graduation: New evidence from Italy. *Research in Higher Education, 60*, 203–218. https://doi.org/10.1007/s11162-018-9512-4

Columbu, S., Porcu, M., Primerano, I., Sulis, I., & Vitale, M. P. (2021). Geography of Italian student mobility: A network analysis approach. *Socio-Economic Planning Sciences, 73*, 100918.

Conti, N., Marangoni, F., & Verzichelli, L. (2020). Euroscepticism in Italy from the onset of the crisis: Tired of Europe? *South European Society and Politics*, 1–26. https://doi.org/10.1080/13608746.2020.1757885

Contini, D., & Salza, G. (2020). Too few university graduates. Inclusiveness and effectiveness of the Italian higher education system. *Socio-Economic Planning Sciences, 71*, 100803.

D'Alimonte, R. (2019). How the populists won in Italy. *Journal of Democracy, 30*(1), 114–127. https://doi.org/10.1353/jod.2019.0009

Dennison, J., & Geddes, A. (2022). The centre no longer holds: The Lega, Matteo Salvini and the remaking of Italian immigration politics. *Journal of Ethnic and Migration Studies, 48*(2), 441–460.

Di Matteo, D., & Mariotti, I. (2021). Italian discontent and right-wing populism: Determinants, geographies, patterns. *Regional Science Policy & Practice, 13*(2), 371–396.

Di Pietro, G. (2012). The Bologna Process and widening participation in university education: New evidence from Italy. *Empirica, 39*(3), 357–374. https://doi.org/10.1007/s10663-011-9172-5

Dobbins, M., Martens, K., Niemann, D., & Vögtle, E. M. (2023). The Bologna Process as a multidimensional architecture of policy diffusion in Western Europe. In *Comparative higher education politics: Policymaking in North America and Western Europe* (pp. 427–453). Springer International Publishing.

Donà, A. (2022). The rise of the radical right in Italy: The case of Fratelli d'Italia. *Journal of Modern Italian Studies, 27*(5), 775–794.

EHEA. (2022). Statement by members and consultative members of the Bologna Follow-up Group on consequences of the Russian invasion of Ukraine. http://ehea. info/Upload/STATEMENT%20BY%20MEMBERS%20AND%20CONSULTAT IVE%20MEMBERS%20OF%20THE%20BOLOGNA%20FOLLOW%20UP%

20GROUP%20ON%20CONSEQUENCES%20OF%20THE%20RUSSIAN%20INVASION%20OF%20UKRAINE.pdf. Accessed on June 14, 2024.

Euronews. (2024, June 10). Italy: PM Meloni established as kingmaker as party secures win in elections. https://www.euronews.com/my-europe/2024/06/10/italy-pm-meloni-established-as-kingmaker-as-party-secures-win-in-elections. Accessed on August 26, 2024.

Frondizi, R., Fantauzzi, C., Colasanti, N., & Fiorani, G. (2019). The evaluation of universities' third mission and intellectual capital: Theoretical analysis and application to Italy. *Sustainability*, *11*(12), 3455. https://doi.org/10.3390/su11123455

Geddes, A., & Pettrachin, A. (2020). Italian migration policy and politics: Exacerbating paradoxes. *Contemporary Italian Politics*, *12*(2), 227–242.

Giannetti, D., Umansky, K., & Sened, I. (2024). The entry of the M5S and the reshaping of party politics in Italy (2008–2018). *Government and Opposition*, *59*(2), 464–481.

Grek, S. (2008). From symbols to numbers: The shifting technologies of education governance in Europe. *European Educational Research Journal*, *7*(2), 208–218. https://doi.org/10.2304/eerj.2008.7.2.208

Guccio, C., Martorana, M. F., & Monaco, L. (2016). Evaluating the impact of the Bologna Process on the efficiency convergence of Italian universities: A non-parametric frontier approach. *Journal of Productivity Analysis*, *45*, 275–298. https://doi.org/10.1007/s11123-015-0459-6

Huisman, J., & Van Der Wende, M. (2004). The EU and Bologna: Are supra- and international initiatives threatening domestic agendas? *European Journal of Education*, *39*(3), 349–357. https://doi.org/10.1111/j.1465-3435.2004.00188.x

Hutter, S., & Kriesi, H. (2020). Politicizing Europe in times of crisis. In J. Zeitlin & F. Nicoli (Eds.), *The European Union beyond the polycrisis?* (pp. 34–55). Routledge.

Jakobi, A. P., & Rusconi, A. (2009). Lifelong learning in the Bologna Process: European developments in higher education. *Compare*, *39*(1), 51–65. https://doi.org/10.1080/03057920801936977

Keating, A. (2009). Educating Europe's citizens: Moving from national to post-national models of educating for European citizenship. *Citizenship Studies*, *13*(2), 135–151.

Kushnir, I. (2016). The role of the Bologna Process in defining Europe. *European Educational Research Journal*, *15*(6), 664–675. https://doi.org/10.1177/1474904116657549

Kushnir, I. (2020). The voice of inclusion in the midst of neoliberalist noise in the Bologna Process. *European Educational Research Journal*, *19*(6), 485–505.

Kushnir, I. (2021). The role of the European Education Area in European Union integration in times of crises. *European Review*, *30*(3), 301–321. https://doi.org/10.1017/S1062798721000016

Kushnir, I. (2022). Referentiality mechanisms in EU education policymaking: The case of the European Education Area. *European Journal of Education*, *57*(1), 128–141.

Kushnir, I., & Yazgan, N. (2023). The politics of higher education: The European Higher Education Area through the eyes of its stakeholders in France and Italy. *Humanities and Social Sciences Communications*, *10*, 774.

Moscati, R. (2009). *The implementation of the Bologna Process in Italy* (pp. 207–225). Springer. https://doi.org/10.1007/978-1-4020-9505-4_9

Nikolayenko, O. (2021). Anti-corruption protests and university students: Evidence from Russian cities. *Government and Opposition*, 1–20. https://doi.org/10.1017/gov.2021.54

Nikolayenko, O. (2023). Gender and repression in an autocracy: Findings from Belarus. *European Journal of Politics and Gender*, 1–22. https://doi.org/10.1332/25151088Y2023D000000011

Nyangau, J. Z. (2014). Higher education as an instrument of economic growth in Kenya. *FIRE: Forum for International Research in Education*, *1*(1), 7–25. https://doi.org/10.18275/fire201401011006

Pasquinucci, D. (2022). From narrative to counter-narrative: The European constraint and the rise of Italian populist Euroscepticism. *Journal of Contemporary European Studies*, *30*(1), 39–51. https://doi.org/10.1080/14782804.2020.1839396

Pastore, F. (2019). Why so slow? The school-to-work transition in Italy. *Studies in Higher Education*, *44*(8), 1358–1371.

Peters, B. (2019). *Institutional theory in political science: The new institutionalism*. Edward Elgar Publishing.

Piromalli, L. (2023). Higher education policy in practice: Digitalisation and the governance reform in an Italian university (1988-2021). *History of Education*, 1–16. https://doi.org/10.1080/0046760X.2022.2141355

Riddervold, M., Trondal, J., &Newsome, A. (Eds.). (2021). *The Palgrave handbook of EU crises*. Palgrave Macmillan.

Robertson, S. L., de Azevedo, M. L. N., & Dale, R. (2016). Higher education, the EU and the cultural political economy of regionalism. In S. L. Robertson, K. Olds, R. Dale, & Q. A. Dang (Eds.), *Global regionalisms and higher education*. Edward Elgar Publishing. https://doi.org/10.4337/9781784712358.00010

Rome Ministerial Communique. (2020). http://www.ehea.info/Upload/Rome_Ministerial_Communique.pdf. Accessed on June 10, 2024.

Ruiu, M. L. (2020). Mismanagement of Covid-19: Lessons learned from Italy. *Journal of Risk Research*, *23*(7–8), 1007–1020.

Sanfelici, M. (2020). The Italian response to the COVID-19 crisis: Lessons learned and future direction in social development. *The International Journal of Community and Social Development*, *2*(2), 191–210.

Santelli, F., Ragozini, G., & Vitale, M. P. (2022). Assessing the effects of local contexts on the mobility choices of university students in Campania region in Italy. *Genus*, *78*(1), 5.

Terzyan, A.(2019). State-building in Belarus: The politics of repression under Lukashenko's rule. Post-Soviet Politics Research Papers. https://doi.org/10.47669/PSRP-2-2019. http://eurasiainstitutes.org/files/file/psprp_n_2_belarus_2019.pdf. Accessed on June 10, 2024.

The Guardian. (2024, February 27). Sardinia elects leftwing president, in blow to Giorgia Meloni. https://www.theguardian.com/world/2024/feb/27/italy-sardinia-elects-leftwing-president-alessandra-todde. Accessed on June 10, 2024.

Ursin, J., Huusko, M., Aittola, H., Kiviniemi, U., & Muhonen, R. (2008). Evaluation and quality assurance in Finnish and Italian universities in the Bologna Process. *Quality in Higher Education*, *14*(2), 109–120. https://doi.org/10.1080/13538320802278222

Vasilopoulou, S., & Talving, L. (2024). Euroscepticism as a syndrome of stagnation? Regional inequality and trust in the EU. *Journal of European Public Policy*, *31*(6), 1494–1515.

Vesperi, W., & Gagnidze, I. (2021). Rethinking the university system: Toward the entrepreneurial university (the case of Italy). *Kybernetes*, *50*(7), 2021–2041.

Zulianello, M. (2022). Italian general election 2022: The populist radical right goes mainstream. *Political Insight*, *13*(4), 20–23.

Chapter 7

United Kingdom's Membership(s) in the European Higher Education Area: Applying a Heterogeneous Agenda

Authored by Iryna Kushnir

Abstract

This chapter focuses on the United Kingdom's two memberships in the European Higher Education Area (EHEA), which represent the final aspects of the collective case study of the EHEA's founders' perspectives regarding the role of European cooperation in higher education, represented by the EHEA initiatives, in Europe. Relying on neo-institutionalism, six in-depth interviews with key UK Bologna stakeholders and their 19 official communications, as well as some international-level EHEA communications, this chapter demonstrates that the two United Kingdom members in the EHEA have had very different views on the role of their memberships in the EHEA and the EHEA in Europe.

Keywords: United Kingdom; Bologna Process; European Higher Education Area; EHEA; Europeanisation; internationalisation; Scotland; EWNI; politics; Europe

7.1 Introduction

This chapter focuses on the United Kingdom (UK) which is the fourth and final element of the collective case study of the European Higher Education Area's (EHEA's) founders' perspectives regarding the role of European cooperation in higher education (HE), illustrated by the EHEA initiatives, in understanding the evolving mission of the European project in the post-2020 period, focusing on the early 2020s.¹ As explained in the introductory Chapter 1, the analysis of the United Kingdom is prompted by a range of gaps in prior relevant research and involves two of the United Kingdom's memberships in the EHEA: one for England, Wales and Northern Ireland, which is presented as 'the United Kingdom' on the EHEA website, and the other one separately for Scotland (EHEA, 2024b). If one is unfamiliar with the context, this may be confusing as the United Kingdom normally represents all four parts of the United Kingdom. For the purpose of this chapter, Birtwistle's (2009, p. 59) abbreviation 'EWNI', which stands for 'The EWNI (England, Wales, Northern Ireland) part of the UK' in the EHEA, is adopted to refer to one of the memberships of United Kingdom's memberships in the United Kingdom. The other UK membership in the EHEA – Scotland – should be self-explanatory in terms of its geopolitical boundaries. The reasons for the two memberships will be explained later in this chapter.

Chapter 2 explained the neo-institutionalist approach which frames the analysis in this book. The methodological decisions that underpin the project, reported in this book, were presented in the introductory Chapter. However, it is worth reminding that the analysis in this chapter rests on a thematic analysis of six in-depth semi-structured elite interviews with an opportunistic/snowball sample of key Bologna stakeholders in both United Kingdom's members in the EHEA, supplemented by 19 official communications from the United Kingdom's Bologna stakeholders.² The interviewees represented the following stakeholders: the Scottish Government (Scotland), Guild HE (England, Wales, N. Ireland and Scotland), the National Union of Students (NUS-UK) (England, Wales, N. Ireland), Universities UK International (England, Wales, N. Ireland), National Union of Students (NUS-Scotland) (Scotland) and another key HE actor in the United Kingdom (Scotland) who wished to keep their organisational affiliation undisclosed. It is also worth reminding that the interviews with the UK stakeholders took place in 2021. This was the first phase of the project which took place a year earlier than the rest of the interviews in the other three founders of the EHEA, discussed in Chapters 4–6. While the timing of the UK interviews did not seem to have an impact on the content of what was discussed, there was one important topic that was omitted from the UK interviews because of their timing. The fact that they took place a few months before the launch of the full-scale attack on Ukraine by Russia meant that the UK stakeholders' responses to the war were not a matter of discussion.

---

¹This chapter is derived in part from an article published in *European Education*, June 28, 2023, copyright CC BY-NC-ND 4.0, published by Routledge, Taylor & Francis Group, Informa Group Plc, available online: Kushnir, I. (2023). Rational-choice neo-institutionalism in Europeanization in the United Kingdom and Germany: A toolkit offered by their memberships in the European Higher Education Area. *European Education*, 55(2), 61–77. http://www.tandfonline.com/10.1080/10564934.2023.2226634

²The dataset with interview transcripts, generated and analysed during the research project that informs this book, is available in the Research Data Archive of Nottingham Trent University, at https://doi.org/10.17631/RD-2022-0001-DDOC.

This chapter starts with explaining recent developments in UK politics particularly with regard to its positionality and attitudes towards the European project. According to historical neo-institutionalism, explained in Chapter 2, this is essential to contextualise the analysis below. This is then followed by a review of literature on the Bologna Process (BP) in the United Kingdom and presenting key findings about UK EHEA stakeholders' perspectives on the role of HE in Europe after 2020.

This chapter demonstrates that the two UK members in the EHEA have had very different views on the role of their memberships in the EHEA and the EHEA in Europe. EWNI, where England's Bologna stakeholders set the tone for work (Kushnir & Brooks, 2022), have been focused on observing the developments in the EHEA and wider politics surrounding it, keeping the HE cooperation ties and looking outwards to cooperating with other regions. EWNI's attitude to the Europeanisation politics of the European region is that of a former empire – willingness to maintain international connections and external influence, while not being an active leader in the EHEA or in the European project. For Scotland, which is the other UK member in the EHEA, HE cooperation in the framework of the EHEA is an instrument for Scotland's politics of Europeanisation, particularly the mending of the ties with the European Union (EU), shaken post-Brexit.

7.2 Recent Developments in UK Politics

Grek and Ozga (2010, p. 941) explain that 'the UK imagined itself to have retained imperial status and looked on the choice of the European "project" as one of many possibilities' before it was 'dragged into a reluctant partnership in Europe.' The authors continue arguing that in the United Kingdom, 'there is a persistent trend among policy actors to respond to questions about international contacts through an amalgamation of European and global influences' (Grek & Ozga, 2010, p. 942). This suggests that the Europeanisation process in the United Kingdom was often steered away from its Europe-rooted nature, acquiring a more general internationalisation flavour. It was possible because Europeanisation could, in fact, be regarded as a regional form of internationalisation which is a more global process based on similar principles (Kehm, 2003).

The nature of Europeanisation in the United Kingdom used to be a matter of a heated debate in the literature on UK politics. Examples include Spiering's (2014) book entitled 'A Cultural History of British Euroscepticism' which elaborates on the United Kingdom's historically wedged position in relation to 'the European'. Such sentiments are also present in Fletcher's (2009, p. 71) analysis of the 'balancing of the United Kingdom's "Ins" and "Outs"' in its membership in the EU. Another similar example is Crescenzi et al.'s (2018, p. 117) discussion of the United Kingdom's 'split Europeanisation' which has increasingly been dominated by Euroscepticism which is 'triggered by the increasing mismatch between internationalized economies (and corporate economic interests) and localistic societies.' However, the devolution in the United Kingdom has facilitated a degree of divergence in these attitudes, with England representing the majority of the Eurosceptic views and Scotland expressing quite strong pro-European attitudes (Hepburn, 2006). This has remained a trend after Brexit, too (Stolz, 2020).

Brexit has seriously questioned the attitude of the United Kingdom towards *the European* in any policy area with European links. Migration linked to the post-2015 refugee crisis and particularly the EU Freedom of Movement and, more generally, tight political and economic links with the EU were the main areas of debate leading up to the Brexit vote. Specifically, Freeden (2017, p. 1) claims that:

> [A]t the height of the crisis of refugees from Syria, Africa and other middle eastern countries, I pointed to one striking difference between sentiments on migration on the European continent and in the UK. In continental Europe, people were afraid of refugees; in the UK, people were afraid of Europeans. Of course, this needs the kind of fine-tuning that a media soundbite cannot provide.

The scholar recognises that the media failed to detail the nuances of the underlying issues. There are also more provocative accounts of the UK Leave Campaign, anchoring on the refugee crisis coupled with the EU Freedom of Movement:

> The Leave Campaign, and particularly UKIP, made immigration a wedge issue in the referendum, one of whose most enduring images was of Nigel Farage standing in front of a billboard-size poster showing an endless line of refugees with the caption: "BREAKING POINT: The EU has failed us all. We must break free of the EU and take back control of our borders." So did Britain's tabloid press, which amplified local horror stories (whether true or false)... Opinion polls repeatedly showed immigration to be a major concern among potential Leave voters. (Sayer, 2017, p. 99)

Ironically, the details of what Brexit would mean for the United Kingdom and the EU started to be worked out following the Brexit vote, making the transitional period between 2016 and 2020 full of uncertainty for both sides. Initially, Brexit had a limited effect on the cooperation with other EU member states (Taggart & Szczerbiak, 2018), perhaps partly because of the challenges in devising a mutually satisfactory deal. The debate about the deal was tremendously complex, working out the details of the choice between 'hard' or 'soft' Brexit. 'Hard Brexit' referred to the position of leaving the EU's Single Market. Soft Brexit referred to staying in the EU's Single Market and Customs Union' (Hobolt, 2018, p. 3). The disagreements existed not only between the EU and the United Kingdom but also within the EU and the United Kingdom (Hobolt, 2018). The difficulties in agreeing a deal may have, arguably, been related to a possible hidden agenda of both parties in using these issues as a reason to eventually retain the United Kingdom's membership in the EU (Kushnir et al., 2020). However, a deal was reached eventually with multiple coming backs about the validity of what has been agreed or needing more clarity on issues such as the Ireland/North Ireland border (Whitten, 2024). A degree of dissatisfaction has been growing with the progression of Brexit in the areas where the 'remain' vote dominated such as, for example, Scotland, as well as even among the slightly bigger part of the UK population that voted for it (51.89%) (Tilley & Hobolt, 2024). Continuing 'resistance to leaving the European Union' dominates in Scotland, especially among the high proportion of EU migrants (Bogacki et al., 2024). It is also worth noting that the post-Brexit negotiations between Scotland and the EU were particularly complex – 'a political minefield' due to 'an absence of political autonomy for Scotland', according to Wright (2018, p. 151).

The post-Brexit UK/EU cooperation in different areas has been full of uncertainties (Martill & Sus, 2021), including HE (Brusenbauch Meislová, 2021), aggravated by the layering of a range of other significant crises. One of them was the COVID-19 pandemic, the pitfalls of handling of which by the conservative government of the United Kingdom has put in deep cracks in the trust of the public in the conservatives (Williams, 2024).These trust issues may have contributed to making them give away power to the Labour Party in Labour's landslide win in securing a majority in the 2024 election (BBC, 2024). Another challenge the United Kingdom has faced jointly with the rest of the European region was the launch of the Russian full-scale invasion of Ukraine in 2022 and the accompanying threat of the spread of the Russian aggression. These issues have consolidated countries in the European region including the United Kingdom in their support of Ukraine and their defence development agenda (Hooghe et al., 2024).

These changes and resulting uncertainties have put the continuation of the Europeanisation in the post-Brexit UK into question.

7.3 The UK and the Bologna Process

Grek et al. (2009) and Grek and Ozga (2010) are among those who investigate Europeanisation in the area of education in the United Kingdom. Their work echoes the England vs Scotland differential attitude to Europeanisation, mentioned earlier. Grek and Ozga (2010, p. 937) emphasise that 'policy-makers in England reference global influences, rather than Europe, while policy-makers in Scotland reference Europe in order to project a new positioning of Scotland in closer alignment with Europe'. The authors also point out that the terms 'the UK', 'Britain' and 'England' are often used interchangeably in the education policy literature, and 'the UK' is often mistakenly understood 'as a unitary state in relation to education' (Grek & Ozga, 2010, p. 939). Interestingly, this still remains the case at least in relation to how the EWNI part of the United Kingdom is still presented on the EHEA website – the 'United Kingdom' (EHEA, 2024b), as if it represented Scotland as well.

While research about UK HE is boundless, the studies that focus specifically on the United Kingdom's participation in the EHEA are limited. Earlier studies are focused on the work of the Bologna action points specifically in England, while acknowledging similarities with other parts of the United Kingdom (Field, 2005; Hartley & Virkus, 2003; Witte & Wright, 2008). Lifelong learning features in the study by Jakobi and Rusconi (2008) who investigated its implementation in the four founding nations of the EHEA, including the United Kingdom as a whole. The authors admit that differences exist in the four parts of the United Kingdom, but they focus on the similarities among the four constituents of the United Kingdom. The promotion of student mobility was perhaps the most attractive EHEA objective for the United Kingdom as a whole, but the United Kingdom's international student market has never been limited to the EHEA (Cemmell & Bekhradnia, 2008). Despite some work associated with the Bologna action points, according to Furlong (2005), overall, the United Kingdom made little effort in response to the call of the EHEA to harmonise HE structures in its signatories. The author uses the terms 'the UK' and 'Britain' interchangeably but seems not to include Scotland in the discussion, which is not admitted explicitly. This can only be inferred based on the statements, such as, 'In Britain the three-year Bachelors is the norm, and most Masters are one year in duration' (Furlong, 2005, p. 59). This statement excludes Scotland, since Bachelor's programs are 4 years long there (Armstrong, 2023). Such limited enthusiasm for Bologna can be partly explained by Witte's (2008) analysis which provides evidence that the UK government assumed that its structures had already been quite similar to what Bologna set out to achieve in the EHEA.

There are only couple of studies that make a clear analytical distinction between EWNI and Scotland in Bologna. Specifically, Birtwistle (2009, p. 59) emphasises EWNI's reluctance to take action in relation to the Bologna action line about the implementation of the European Credit Transfer System,

> The EWNI (England, Wales, Northern Ireland) part of the UK is shown as being regarded as weak in its use and implementation of the European Credit Transfer and Accumulation System (ECTS)... whereas Scotland is shown as having strength in this area.

Some aspects of the project presented in this book were also published in Kushnir and Brooks (2022) and Kushnir (2023) which follow Birtwistle's terminology for the distinction of the two United Kingdom's membership in the EHEA.

One strand of more recent studies – from the last decade – elaborates more on the idea of the lack of interest in Bologna. Marquand and Scott (2018) focus on England and Wales, stating that the BP was 'largely ignored' there in comparison to EU countries. Similarly, Sin (2012, p. 393) summarises England's response to Bologna as 'academic disconnection and missing leadership' and Sin and Saunders (2014, pp. 531–532) nominate England's approach to Bologna as 'selective acquiescence', pointing at 'concerns raised in political circles that perceived and pictured the Bologna Process more like a threat (bureaucracy, top-down enforcement, infringing institutional autonomy) than an opportunity.' Another strand of recent studies explores Bologna in the United Kingdom in more indirect ways, meaning not directly focused on or linked to Bologna action points, which, ironically, confirms the lack of interest in the UK Bologna, = per se. Examples include: the work of Raffe (2011a, 2011b) on the National Qualifications Framework in Scotland which is encouraged by Bologna but the impact of Bologna on the policy process in Scotland is not emphasised, studies about student mobility to and from the United Kingdom through Erasmus+ which is a supporting pillar of Bologna action lines (Brooks, 2021a; Ploner & Nada, 2019; Zotti, 2021), Brooks' (2021b) understanding of 'the student' that is constructed in the context of European policy in England in comparison to a selection of five EU countries.

UK cooperation with European HE partners post-Brexit has been gaining momentum recently as well (Brooks & Waters, 2023; Brusenbauch Meislová, 2021; Courtois & Veiga, 2020; Highman, 2019). Initial analysis of UK HE cooperation initiatives in the framework of the new Turing programme which has replaced Erasmus+ in the effort to set UK HE up for more global connections rather than focusing on European connections (Brooks & Waters, 2023) are of a particular importance.

This chapter builds on a couple of papers (Kushnir, 2023; Kushnir & Brooks, 2022) related to the project discussed in this book. It addresses a range of overlapping gaps in the scholarship about Bologna in the United Kingdom: the distinction between the memberships of EWNI and Scotland and the role they play in constructing the United Kingdom's overarching agenda in HE, the United Kingdom's reasons for maintaining its EHEA membership specifically in the post-Brexit climate and the place of Europeanisation, if any, in this context. The state of affairs in the early 2020s is of a special interest here because 2020 marks a 'tipping point' for the EHEA countries. In addition to the change of European geopolitics in 2020 following the end of Brexit transitional period, the year 2020 was the deadline for the achievement of a 'fully-functioning EHEA' (EHEA, 2024b) and planning further work.

7.4 A Passive, yet Complex, Role of the United Kingdom's Memberships in the European Higher Education Area and the Politics of Europeanisation and Internationalisation

The analysis of the interviews and official communications from key EHEA stakeholders in Scotland and EWNI has revealed a more inward-looking view of the role of their HE cooperation with others in the framework of the EHEA. The discussion below focuses specifically on what we can learn about the United Kingdom's stakeholders more passive, albeit still complex, role in the EHEA compared to the other three members, discussed in the previous chapters, as well as the link of this to the United Kingdom's politics of Europeanisation and internationalisation.

7.4.1 The Complexity of the Two Memberships

Before delving into the analysis of each of the UK memberships, an important point to raise regarding the United Kingdom's memberships in the EHEA is about the lack of clarity about who exactly in the United Kingdom was among the initiators of the EHEA. There is a discrepancy in relevant references in the literature. A large group of scholars state that the United Kingdom along with Germany, France and Italy signed the Sorbonne Declaration in 1998 (e.g. Furlong, 2005; Jakobi & Rusconi, 2009; Matei et al., 2018; Torotcoi, 2017). There is, however, another smaller group of scholars who refer to England in place of the United Kingdom in this list (e.g. Cemmell & Bekhradnia, 2008; Erkoç & Bayrakçi, 2017; Zmas, 2015). Sorbonne Declaration (1998) details that Tessa Blackstone was the minister who represented the United Kingdom as a whole, despite being affiliated with the English administration.

The second and even more important point to clarify is the United Kingdom's two memberships in the EHEA. As specified in Chapter 1, the membership for EWNI is presented as 'the United Kingdom' on the EHEA website, and the other membership is separately for Scotland (EHEA, 2024a). If one is unfamiliar with the context, this may be confusing as the United Kingdom represents all four parts of the United Kingdom including Scotland. The reasons for the two memberships require explanation. This should be attributed to a range of differences that the HE systems in Scotland and the rest of the United Kingdom have had. An example of this is a common three-year undergraduate degree in EWNI, while in Scotland an undergraduate degree lasts four years (Sweeney, 2010). The Scottish education system at all levels has always been different, and the Scotland Act of 1998 created reserved powers for Scotland, HE being one of them, and further institutionalised those differences (Gallacher & Raffe, 2012). Separate EHEA memberships, arguably, are an expression of those differences. No details about the timing and context of the emergence of the dual membership of the United Kingdom in the EHEA are provided in scholarly literature, neither is it explained on the EHEA website. Nevertheless, a representative of the Scottish government, interviewed in the framework of this project, has shed a glimpse of light on this matter:

> Scotland's distinct position within the EHEA/the Bologna Process arose due to Scotland's education system being fully devolved, and Scottish officials and ministers being needed to provide advice on the Scottish system as relates to e.g. quality assurance and academic recognition (which of course was highly relevant back when the EHEA was founded). There is no, to the best of my knowledge, formal Bologna document which spells out the peculiarities of the UK's participation within the EHEA: this is instead... an internal UK matter which has been accommodated within the structures of the EHEA/Bologna Process in the same way that Belgium has both its Flemish and French communities represented in the Process. I imagine that back in the day when the structures of the EHEA were first being created there will have

been internal discussions within the UK about how to best ensure Scotland's education system was represented, which then led to a Scottish representative taking one of the UK's two seats (to note that, of course, all countries have two seats and others use them in different ways that suit them e.g. Germany having a federal and rotating state seat). (A4)

The degree of interaction between the two memberships of the United Kingdom in Bologna has not been static. For example, reports submitted by EWNI and Scotland prior to 2005 do not make a formal distinction between the two memberships, such as in the 'National Report United Kingdom 2003' (EHEA, 2024c, 2024d). The same report features both on the EWNI and Scotland pages of the EHEA website, but it does make 29 references on its 10-page length to the peculiarities of Bologna implementation in Scotland in addition to how it worked in the rest of the United Kingdom (EHEA, 2024c, 2024d). All subsequent reports on the EWNI and Scotland on the EHEA website are different. However, this is not to say that there have been no more joint relevant documents (see Table 3 in Chapter 1). A degree of overlaps in the remit and functioning of the memberships of EWNI and Scotland in the EHEA should be acknowledged based on the fact that they are part of one country, with their respective devolved administrations working closely together in governing different matters including HE (Gallacher & Raffe, 2012). However, the differences have been sufficient enough to maintain two separate memberships in the EHEA, detailed below.

7.4.2 EWNI

The continuing EHEA membership of EWNI is driven predominantly by the English administration and is explained by the stakeholders in terms of power-related incentives but also economic profit incentives, both of which are related to HE specifically and to Westminster's wider politics of internationalisation. Historical neo-institutionalism serving as a contextual background in this discussion (rather than the focus) dictates the need to appeal to the legacy of English imperialism. Choosing not to be actively involved in the Europeanisation driven by the EU historically (Crescenzi et al., 2018) would pre-empt us from being taken by surprise by what a representative from Guild HE has shared:

> ...we've always tried to use our engagement with the Bologna Process as a way of influencing them, rather than them influencing us. (A1)

The 'us-them' distinction here refers to EWNI vs the rest of the EHEA. Such a distinction and the idea of passively observing the developments in the EHEA with an opportunity to make EWNI's voice heard if needed is a common theme in the interviews with the Bologna stakeholders from the United Kingdom. EWNI's HE international strategy is an important pillar in the support of the United Kingdom's wider power politics of internationalisation summarised well in the following extract from the *International Education Strategy* (Department for Education and Department for International Trade, 2021): 'It is paramount that the government continues to develop the UK's soft power globally.'

The assumed rational choice-making process of such a power position may also shed more light on the lack of interest in making any substantial changes in the HE sector in response to the BP, evident from prior research in the field in this context (e.g. Marquand & Scott, 2018). This reserved attitude to the EHEA is also present in the policy paper *International Education Strategy* (Department for Education and Department for International Trade, 2021), which is a key strategic document for driving HE development in the country. No explicit references are present to the BP or the EHEA in this document. Nevertheless, the BP does feature implicitly in this key document in the references to quality assurance and internationalisation, and a mutually shaping relationship between HE politics and the wider politics of internationalisation is evident.

In addition to the power rationales for continuing EWNI's EHEA membership presently, despite Brexit and leaving Erasmus+, economic motivations are also rationalised in the data. The representative from GuildHE also points out economic advantages for EWNI in staying part of the EHEA, which is illustrative of similar opinions expressed by other interviewees, both in EWNI and Scotland. Such a partly consumerist position of EWNI is related first and foremost to student mobility which the EHEA facilitates beyond the Erasmus+ Programme (e.g. in the form of other exchanges through partnership agreements and recognition frameworks):

> ...it's been more of an observer role for the UK [EWNI]... Stand back, watch, and see what happens, and take from it the bits that it's particularly interested in... what we would call, a bit-part player... there are times when it's better to do things collectively and to be seen to be a cooperative, interested player. (A2, a representative of a key HE actor from Scotland)

It is also worth explaining further the earlier mentioned point about England's administration driving the strategy of EWNI's membership in the EHEA. First, the government official communications that were analysed all find their origin in the central UK government which is driven by the English administration (Department for Business, Energy and Industrial Strategy, 2019; Department for Education, 2019a, 2019b, Department for Education and Department for International Trade, 2021). The headquarters of the other organisations whose official communications related to EWNI membership in the EHEA were reviewed (see Table 3 in Chapter 1) are all located in England, which suggests more input and influence from English voices – Quality Assurance Agency in Gloucester, Universities UK International and the Association of Colleges both in London (Association of Colleges, 2022; Quality Assurance Agency, 2022; Universities UK, 2022). A key HE actor from Scotland summarises who drives the EWNI membership in the EHEA which is presented as 'the United Kingdom' on the EHEA website (EHEA, 2024d):

> ...historically, the UK has a place [in the EHEA], but it's actually 'UK-England'. (A2)

The fact that the focus of prior literature on the BP in the United Kingdom is specifically on England (e.g. Sin, 2012; Sin & Saunders, 2014) may be justified by England's leading role in the HE policymaking in EWNI. This would also resonate with the power dynamics in policymaking in the United Kingdom beyond HE (Gallacher & Raffe, 2012).

Moreover, the HE sector of N. Ireland had a hard time accepting Brexit and the resulting departure from Erasmus+ (Koch, 2021), similar to Scotland, as explained below. However, while Scotland's voice in the EHEA becomes clear due to its separate EHEA membership, the voice of N. Ireland gets lost in a specifically EHEA discussion in the context of N. Ireland's joint membership with England and Wales. While its voice seems to be subdued in the official communications that have been analysed, the interview data bring it up, opposing it as well as Wales' voice to that of England with regard to the development of social justice in HE:

> In England, with the Office for Students, there is a baseline set of regulations to get on the register, and you either comply or you don't comply... Whereas in the Nations, that's the opposite, we believe that that's not enough. You need to help people to improve. (A2, a key HE actor from Scotland)

These issues bring us right back to where the discussion in this section started – England administration's leading role in the EWNI membership and the power ambitions at stake. Evidently, they are relevant not just with regard to the EHEA context broadly but are also linked to the BP management within the United Kingdom. Additionally, the question of Wales' separate seat in the EHEA has been raised but this has not led to any changes to the EWNI membership:

> Occasionally, the Welsh will say, can we not get our own seat on this as well? Or, how best can we have Welsh issues raised within this process? And that answer is never really fully addressed, partly because there is a limited number of seats or places that a country can have within the process. (A4, representative of the Scottish Government)

7.4.3 Scotland

'Scotland's very distinct education system' was likely to offer Scotland a chance to get their 'foot in the door at the beginning' by securing a separate membership in the EHEA (A4, representative of the Scottish Government). Scotland's membership is more uniform in the EHEA due to having one nation in it unlike the power imbalance between the nations in EWNI, discussed above. Among different reasons, Scotland's continuing EHEA membership is rationalised, first and foremost, by the need to mend its relationship with Europe inevitably caused by Brexit, both in HE and beyond, with 'the European Union: protecting Scotland's place in Europe' being set out as a key objective in the *Scotland's International Framework* (Scottish Government, 2017). The BP is not explicitly mentioned in this overarching framework which covers all areas of policy, but European cooperation in education and research is emphasised there.

The interviewees representing Scottish Bologna stakeholders believe strongly in the value of the BP for the development of Scottish HE which shares a lot in common with the HE in other European countries, and they recognise that the link to the EHEA now is particularly valuable to demonstrate to the rest of the EHEA the value of the BP and European connections for Scotland. Here are a couple of illustrative quotes to evidence this:

> ...the Scots have always loved Bologna. They've always wanted to be very engaged with it. They hate the fact that we left the European Union, therefore I can imagine them wanting to get even more engaged [in the EHEA] in the future... Scotland would want to be part of the European community. So, anything that's like that [involving European cooperation], it would want to be part of. (A1, representative from GuildHE)

> The Scottish higher education system is distinctly European, in a way that the UK [excluding Scotland] system is perhaps not as much... the EHEA is a way for us to maintain that European connection. We... have a fear or a concern being outside of the EU... being outside of the EU, we risk being sidelined as the EU seeks to harmonise more of its own higher education policies. Being in the EHEA, while it's not the same as that, it does provide a bit of a link. It's at least something to keep us in the loop as to what's going on... Within Scotland, we have always taken note of our specific presence within the EHEA and the Bologna Process. So, Scotland has been probably a little bit more active than other devolved governments. (A4, representative of the Scottish Government)

Scotland does not seem to hold a strong leading role within the EHEA due to finding itself in the circumstances whereby it has to do a catching-up job. The harmonisation of HE policy in the EU that the representative of the Scottish Government mentions above refers to the well-known European Education Area initiative limited to EU countries only (Kushnir, 2021, 2022). The motivation to stay in tune with the developments in EU HE is vital for Scotland to mend and sustain the European connections established prior to Brexit:

Scotland's higher education institutes have the greatest proportional number of European staff and students there than the rest of the United Kingdom. We have, I think, a greater number of research collaborations per head with Europe than other institutions in the United Kingdom (A4, a representative of the Scottish Government).

Despite this interest in the BP in Scotland and its resulting supposedly equal role in Bologna, the connections to EWNI and a degree of influence of the English administration in the Scottish membership should not be overlooked. Evidently, the interconnectedness between HE stakeholders for EWNI and Scotland is in their structure – while a lot of them would have a Scotland branch such as, for example, NUS-Scotland associated with NUS-UK, some organisations are universal for the whole of the United Kingdom such as Guild HE (EHEA, 2024c, 2024d).

7.4.4 Europeanisation and Internationalisation Associated With the EHEA in the United Kingdom

The data from EWNI and Scotland have evidenced a deliberate and rational inward-looking approach of their stakeholders to continuing their EHEA memberships in order to be able to draw certain benefits. In Graziano and Vink's (2017) terms, the two United Kingdom's memberships in the EHEA can be viewed as a resource that enables all the devolved nations to participate in a form of Europeanisation in HE after Brexit with the aim to draw economic gains, power enhancement and other ideological and political benefits. According to Graziano and Vink (2017, p. 40), resulting 'strategic organizational adaptation displayed by interest groups…when domestic political actors "rationally" use European resources in order to support predefined preferences.' These predefined preferences have appeared to be quite different for the two UK members of the EHEA.

Europeanisation in Scotland turns out to be a regional form of internationalisation, in Kehm's (2003) terms, focused on European values and principles. Scotland's membership in the EHEA is driven by a strong interest in the affiliation and cooperation with European countries. Scotland's aspirations to continue Europeanisation post-2020 through its EHEA membership are an attempt to mend the damages caused by Brexit in the overall UK–EU relationship. Contrastingly, Europeanisation in EWNI seems to be taking more of the form of internationalisation, focusing on the global arena where specifically Europeanisation motives are far from being a primary concern. Europeanisation in EWNI resembles covert internationalisation. Clearly, this is a trend preserved from over a decade ago when Grek and Ozga (2010) explained how policymakers in Scotland referred to European matters more while those in England relied more on references to the global arena in justifying policy choices.

Although the changes and resulting uncertainties that Brexit brought about have put the continuation of Europeanisation in the post-Brexit UK into question, this chapter demonstrates the role of United Kingdom's EHEA memberships in sustaining Europeanisation after the end of the Brexit transitional period in 2020, but in very peculiar forms. There also is a very strong link between the nature of Europeanisation in HE and the wider politics of Europeanisation.

In addition to these more inward-looking accounts of the role of the EHEA – in the United Kingdom – it is also important to point out the insights the above analysis has given us about the United Kingdom's Bologna stakeholders' ideas about the role of the EHEA in Europe. While the UK stakeholders' answers were noticeably less-outward looking (i.e. considering the role of EHEA cooperation for Europe in general) compared to the other three cases presented in the previous Chapters, it is clear that both EWNI and Scotland position the cooperation in the framework of the EHEA as an indispensable internationalisation process in the European region. While EWNI present its importance as equal to their cooperation with other regions, Scotland's strong emphasis on the importance of particularly European cooperation in Europe is palpable.

7.5 Conclusion

Chapter 7 has focused on the United Kingdom's two members of the EHEA which represent the final elements in the collective case study of the EHEA's founders' perspectives on the role of European HE represented by EHEA initiatives in the evolving mission of the European project post-2020. The chapter provided an overview of the United Kingdom's politics particularly related to Europeanisation trends as this is important to contextualise the analysis linked to the EHEA. This was followed by a review of literature on the BP and the United Kingdom and presenting key findings. This chapter has shown that the two UK members in the EHEA have had quite different perspectives on the role of their memberships in the EHEA and the role of the EHEA in Europe more generally.

The next chapter will refer to the findings above in relation to the findings from Germany, France and Italy and discuss them jointly in light of the theoretical and empirical literature on the topic. It will also explain how this book addresses the gaps in this prior literature, which were detailed in Chapters 1 and 3.

References

Armstrong, S. (2023). Crisis or opportunity? International income growth in Scottish universities during Covid-19. *Scottish Affairs, 32*(4), 425–448.
Association of Colleges. (2022). https://www.aoc.co.uk/. Accessed on August 27, 2024.
BBC. (2024, July 5). Labour wins general election. https://www.bbc.co.uk/newsround/articles/cxx2pd3r538o. Accessed on July 8, 2024.
Birtwistle, T. (2009). Towards 2010 (and then beyond) —The context of the Bologna Process. *Assessment in Education: Principles, Policy & Practice, 16*(1), 55–63.
Bogacki, M., Botterill, K., Burrell, K., & Hörschelmann, K. (2024). What about Europe? European identity and spatial imaginaries of Europe among Polish migrants during post-Brexit negotiations in Scotland. *European Urban and Regional Studies, 31*(1), 65–80.

Brooks, R. (2021a). Europe as spatial imaginary? Narratives from higher education 'policy influencers' across the continent. *Journal of Education Policy*, *36*(2), 159–178.

Brooks, R. (2021b). The construction of higher education students within national policy: A cross-European comparison. *Compare: A Journal of Comparative and International Education*, *51*(1), 1–20.

Brooks, R., & Waters, J. (2023). An analysis of the UK's Turing Scheme as a response to socio-economic and geo-political challenges. *Higher Education*, *88*, 1809–1827. https://doi.org/10.1007/s10734-023-00995-0

Brusenbauch Meislová, M. (2021). Lost in the noise? Narrative (re) presentation of higher education and research during the Brexit process in the UK. *European Journal of English Studies*, *25*(1), 34–48.

Cemmell, J., & Bekhradnia, B. (2008). *The Bologna Process and the UK's international student market*. Higher Education Policy Institute.

Courtois, A., & Veiga, A. (2020). Brexit and higher education in Europe: The role of ideas in shaping internationalisation strategies in times of uncertainty. *Higher Education*, *79*(5), 811–827.

Crescenzi, R., Di Cataldo, M., & Faggian, A. (2018). Internationalized at work and localistic at home: The 'split' Europeanization behind Brexit. *Papers in Regional Science*, *97*(1), 117–132.

Department for Business. (2019). Energy and industrial strategy. https://www.gov.uk/government/publications/uk-international-research-and-innovation-strategy/international-research-and-innovation-strategy-webpage. Accessed on August 27, 2024.

Department for Education. (2019a). https://www.gov.uk/government/speeches/universities-minister-gives-speech-at-universities-uk-conference. Accessed on August 27, 2024.

Department for Education. (2019b). https://www.gov.uk/government/speeches/minister-skidmore-my-vision-for-global-higher-education. Accessed on August 27, 2024.

Department for Education and Department for International Trade. (2021). International education strategy (2021 update): Supporting recovery, driving growth. https://www.gov.uk/government/publications/international-education-strategy-2021-update/international-education-strategy-2021-update-supporting-recovery-driving-growth. Accessed on August 27, 2024.

EHEA. (2024a). Full members. https://ehea.info/page-full_members. Accessed on July 2, 2024.

EHEA. (2024b). How does the Bologna Process work. https://ehea.info/page-how-does-the-bologna-process-work. Accessed on July 2, 2024.

EHEA. (2024c). United Kingdom (Scotland). https://ehea.info/page-united-kingdom-scotland. Accessed on July 2, 2024.

EHEA. (2024d). United Kingdom. https://ehea.info/page-united-kingdom. Accessed on July 2, 2024.

Erkoç, Ç., & Bayrakçi, M. (2017). An examination of masters and doctoral dissertations regarding Bologna Process in Turkey on the dimensions of quality. *The Online Journal of Quality in Higher Education*, *4*(2), 19–41.

Field, J. (2005). Bologna and an established system of bachelor's/master's degrees: The example of adult education in Britain. *Bildung und Erziehung*, *58*(2), 207–220.

Fletcher, M. (2009). Schengen, the European Court of justice and flexibility under the Lisbon treaty: Balancing the United Kingdom's 'Ins' and 'Outs'. *European Constitutional Law Review, 5*(1), 71–98.

Freeden, M. (2017). After the Brexit referendum: Revisiting populism as an ideology. *Journal of Political Ideologies, 22*(1), 1–11.

Furlong, P. (2005). British higher education and the Bologna Process: An interim assessment. *Politics, 25*(1), 53–61.

Gallacher, J., & Raffe, D. (2012). Higher education policy in post-devolution UK: More convergence than divergence? *Journal of Education Policy, 27*(4), 467–490.

Graziano, P., & Vink, M. (2017). Europeanization: Concept, theory, and methods. In S. Bulmer & C. Lequesne (Eds.), *The member states of the European Union* (2nd ed.). Oxford University Press.

Grek, S., Lawn, M., Lingard, B., Ozga, J., Rinne, R., Segerholm, C., & Simola, H. (2009). National policy brokering and the construction of the European Education Space in England, Sweden, Finland and Scotland. *Comparative Education, 45*(1), 5–21.

Grek, S., & Ozga, J. (2010). Governing education through data: Scotland, England and the European education policy space. *British Educational Research Journal, 36*(6), 937–952.

Hartley, R. J., & Virkus, S. (2003). Approaches to quality assurance and accreditation of LIS programmes: Experiences from Estonia and United Kingdom. *Education for Information, 21*(1), 31–48.

Hepburn, E. (2006). Scottish autonomy and European Integration: The response of Scotland's political parties. In J. McGarry & M. Keating (Eds.), *European integration and the nationalities question* (pp. 241–254). Routledge.

Highman, L. (2019). Future EU–UK research and higher education cooperation at risk: What is at stake? *Tertiary Education and Management, 25*(1), 45–52.

Hobolt, S. B. (2018). Brexit and the 2017 UK general election. *JCMS: Journal of Common Market Studies, 56*, 39.

Hooghe, L., Marks, G., Bakker, R., Jolly, S., Polk, J., Rovny, J., ... Vachudova, M. A. (2024). The Russian threat and the consolidation of the West: How populism and EU-skepticism shape party support for Ukraine. *European Union Politics, 25*, 459–482.

Jakobi, A. P., & Rusconi, A. (2008). Opening of higher education? A lifelong learning perspective on the Bologna Process. *Compare: A Journal of Comparative and International Education, 39*(1), 51–65.

Jakobi, A. P., & Rusconi, A. (2009). Lifelong learning in the Bologna Process: European developments in higher education. *Compare, 39*(1), 51–65.

Kehm, B. M. (2003). Internationalisation in higher education: From regional to global. In R. Begg (Ed.), *The dialogue between higher education research and practice* (pp. 109–119). Springer.

Koch, K. (2021). Cross-border resilience in higher education: Brexit and its impact on Irish-Northern Irish university cross-border cooperation. In D. J. Andersen & E.-K. Prokkola (Eds.), *Borderlands resilience* (pp. 37–53). Routledge.

Kushnir, I. (2021). The role of the European Education Area in European Union integration in times of crises. *European Review, 30*, 1–2.

Kushnir, I. (2022). Referentiality mechanisms in EU education policymaking: The case of the European Education Area. *European Journal of Education*. https://doi.org/10.1111/ejed.12485

Kushnir, I. (2023). *Rational-choice neo-institutionalism in Europeanization in the UK and Germany: A toolkit offered by their memberships in the European higher education area*. European Education.

Kushnir, I., & Brooks, R. (2022). UK membership(s) in the European Higher Education Area post-2020: A 'Europeanisation' agenda. *European Educational Research Journal, 22*, 718–740.

Marquand, J., & Scott, P. (2018). United Kingdom: England (and Wales up to 1999)—Aesop's hare. In *Democrats, authoritarians and the Bologna Process* (pp. 127–161). Emerald Publishing Limited.

Martill, B., & Sus, M. (2021). *When politics trumps strategy: UK–EU security collaboration after Brexit*. International Political Science Review.

Matei, L., Craciun, D., & Torotcoi, S. (2018). A resounding success or downright failure? Understanding policy transfer within the Bologna Process in Central and Eastern Europe. In A. Batory, A. Cartwright, & D. Stone (Eds.), *Policy experiments, failures and innovations* (pp. 206–224). Edward Elgar Publishing.

Ploner, J., & Nada, C. (2019). International student migration and the postcolonial heritage of European higher education: Perspectives from Portugal and the UK. *Higher Education, 80*, 373–389.

Quality Assurance Agency. (2022). Home. https://www.qaa.ac.uk/#. Accessed on August 27, 2024.

Raffe, D. (2011a). Are 'communications frameworks' more successful? Policy learning from the Scottish credit and qualifications framework. *Journal of Education and Work, 24*(3–4), 283–302.

Raffe, D. (2011b). The role of learning outcomes in national qualifications frameworks. In *Validierung von Lernergebnisse [Recognition and validation of learning outcomes]* (pp. 87–104). BIBB.

Sayer, D. (2017). White riot—Brexit, Trump, and post-factual politics. *The Journal of Historical Sociology, 30*(1), 92–106. https://doi.org/10.1111/johs.12153

Scottish Government. (2017). Scotland's international framework. https://www.gov.scot/publications/scotlands-international-framework-9781788514033/pages/3/. Accessed on August 28, 2024.

Sin, C. (2012). Academic understandings of and responses to Bologna: A three-country perspective. *European Journal of Education, 47*(3), 392–404.

Sin, C., & Saunders, M. (2014). Selective acquiescence, creative commitment and strategic conformity: Situated national policy responses to Bologna. *European Journal of Education, 49*(4), 529–542.

Spiering, M. (2014). *A cultural history of British euroscepticism*. Springer.

Stolz, K. (2020). Scotland, Brexit and the broken promise of democracy. In M. Guderjan, H. Mackay, & G. Stedman (Eds.), *Contested Britain: Brexit, austerity and agency* (p. 189). Bristol University Press.

Sweeney, S. (2010). *Bologna process: Responding to the post-2010 challenge*. Higher Education Academy.

Taggart, P., & Szczerbiak, A. (2018). Putting Brexit into perspective: The effect of the Eurozone and migration crises and Brexit on euroscepticism in European states. *Journal of European Public Policy, 25*(8), 1194–1214. https://doi.org/10.1080/13501763.2018.1467955

Tilley, J., & Hobolt, S. B. (2024). Losers' consent and emotions in the aftermath of the Brexit referendum. *West European Politics, 47*(5), 1180–1198.

Torotcoi, S. (2017). Politics and policies of higher education: Policy transfer and the Bologna Process. *Journal of Research in Higher Education, 1*(2), 6–30.

Universities UK. (2022). Home: Universities UK international. https://www.universitiesuk.ac.uk/universities-uk-international. Accessed on August 27, 2024.

Whitten, L. C. (2024). *Brexit and the Northern Ireland constitution.* Oxford University Press.

Williams, B. (2024). The 'New Right' and its legacy for British conservatism. *Journal of Political Ideologies, 29*(1), 121–144.

Witte, J. (2008). Aspired convergence, cherished diversity: Dealing with the contradictions of Bologna. *Tertiary Education and Management, 14*(2), 81–93.

Wright, A. (2018). Scotland and the EU: All bark and no bite? In A. Wright (Ed.), *Scotland: The challenge of devolution* (pp. 151–163). Routledge.

Zmas, A. (2015). Global impacts of the Bologna Process: International perspectives, local particularities. *Compare: A Journal of Comparative and International Education, 45*(5), 727–747.

Zotti, S. (2021). Academic mobility after Brexit: Erasmus and the UK post-2020. *European Journal of English Studies, 25*(1), 19–33.

Chapter 8

European Cooperation in Higher Education and the Evolving Mission of the European Project (in the Early 2020s)

Authored by Iryna Kushnir

Abstract

This chapter integrates and further discusses the findings from the previous four chapters regarding the perspectives of key higher education actors in the founding countries of the European Higher Education Area (Germany, France, Italy and the United Kingdom) on the strategic significance of their memberships in this Area for them, as well as for the European region. This chapter builds on these findings to analyse the role of European cooperation in higher education for the developing mission of the European project, particularly in the early 2020s period. In doing so, this chapter summarises and develops explicit answers to the key research questions that this book set out to answer. The discussion in this chapter relies on the theoretical and empirical literature outlined earlier in the book and demonstrates how this book addresses relevant gaps in the scholarship on European higher education and the European project.

Keywords: Higher education; European Higher Education Area; EHEA; European project; Europeanisation; European cooperation

8.1 Introduction

This chapter integrates and further discusses the findings in the previous four chapters which presented each of the four cases, namely Germany, France, Italy and the United Kingdom (UK). In doing so, this chapter summarises and

---

European Cooperation in Higher Education, 107–119
Copyright © 2025 Iryna Kushnir.
Published by Emerald Publishing Limited. This work is published under the Creative Commons Attribution (CC BY 4.0) licence. Anyone may reproduce, distribute, translate and create derivative works of this book (for both commercial and non-commercial purposes), subject to full attribution to the original publication and authors. The full terms of this licence may be seen at http://creativecommons.org/licences/by/4.0/legalcode
doi:10.1108/978-1-83753-516-320251021

develops explicit answers to the key research questions that this book set out to answer. To remind, they include:

> What is the role of European cooperation in higher education (HE), represented by the European Higher Education Area, for the evolving mission of the European project in the early 2020s era?
>
> (1) What are the perspectives of key HE actors in the four founding countries of the European Higher Education Area (EHEA) on the strategic significance of their memberships in this Area for them, as well as for the European region?
> (2) How do these findings inform our understanding of the European project?

The discussion in this chapter relies on the theoretical and empirical literature outlined earlier in the book and demonstrates how this book addresses the three main overlapping gaps in the scholarship on European HE and the European project. First of all, this book presents the only study about the four founders of the European Higher Education Area (EHEA), focusing on the interrelation between their EHEA membership agendas and wider politics. However, it is worth mentioning my recent co-authored article on the geopolitics of the European HE space (Kushnir & Yazgan, 2024) which has come out from the same project, beginning the discussion about the four founders of the EHEA. Second, the study presented in this book addresses a temporal and contextual gap in the available scholarship on the intersection between the EHEA and the European project by covering the current period – after the 2020 deadline for the achievement of a fully functioning EHEA, after the end of the Brexit transitional period and the start of a full-scale Russia–Ukraine war. Finally, being informed by neo-institutionalism (NI), this book highlights an innovative theoretical angle in the analysis of Europeanisation politics particularly in the context of EHEA memberships.

By explicating the answers to the research questions, this chapter also consolidates key aspects of the main argument of this book: European cooperation in HE, illustrated in this book by the EHEA, is an instrumental platform for the meaning-making process of the European project's mission which has increasingly been gaining momentum in supporting political stability in the European region, particularly after 2020. The stakeholders in each of the EHEA's founders, despite having different priorities and visions regarding their memberships within the EHEA and EHEA's role in Europe, have all been contributing to the crafting of the purpose of the European project, which has increasingly been transcending the borders of the European Union (EU). This purpose has been to serve an insurer of stability and/or cross-country dialogue.

8.2 Membership in the EHEA: Strategic Significance

This section integrates the findings from Chapters 4–7 and answers the first specific research question about the perspectives of key HE actors in the four founding countries of the EHEA on the strategic significance of their memberships in this area for them, as well as for the European region.

Bergan and Matei (2020, p. 361) questioned whether the EHEA was a '*Fata Morgana* or Continuing Policy Journey.' This was back at the time when the 2020 Rome Conference took place which took stock of what was achieved in the EHEA by its 2020 deadline, with everyone anticipating seeing what would come next. The work on the EHEA was not wrapped up as some may have anticipated (e.g. Gareis & Broekel, 2022; Mendick & Peters, 2022; Pires Pereira et al., 2023), but rather new goals for the EHEA were set – to become 'inclusive, innovative and interconnected' (EHEA, 2020, p. 3). The discussion below demonstrates that, in fact, the EHEA remains, in Bergan and Matei's terms (2020, p. 361) a 'Continuing Policy Journey' due to its strategic significance for the EHEA's signatories as well as for the European region more broadly.

Continuing memberships of Germany, France, Italy and the United Kingdom in the EHEA bare strategic significance for each of these members, as 'rationalised' by their EHEA stakeholders to use the language of the rational-choice strand of NI (Peters, 2019, p. 55). As demonstrated in Chapters 4–7, Germany and France rely on their EHEA memberships to cooperate in leading the development of the European region, with Germany taking a more active role, while France has been performing more of a moderating role in this process. Similarly to Germany and France, Italy also takes a leading role in Europe, albeit the main difference is that its emphasis has been on the HE reforms across the region per se and attempts not to recognise the unavoidably political nature of these reforms. The United Kingdom's case is different from all three in that, first, it has got two members in the EHEA (England, Wales and Northern Ireland (EWNI) and Scotland) with diverging agendas regarding their relations with the rest of Europe. Second, both EWNI's and Scotland's motives for their EHEA memberships seem to be considerably more self-centred as opposed to Germany's, France's and Italy's aspirations for leading others in the European region. Each of these four cases is discussed in more detail below.

Germany, despite its federal structure and in line with its leading role in the Europeanisation processes in the EU and beyond (Caporaso, 2021), views its EHEA membership, first and foremost, as a tool for Europeanisation and for generating and maintaining political stability in the European region. The Russian attack on Ukraine seems to have reignited in the German vision of Europeanisation what Polyakova (2016) sees as the faded peace-building rhetoric. This sense of responsibility for Europe and the positioning of the EHEA as a platform for facilitating international friendships is peculiar to Germany, although France has been sharing and supporting this vision.

France's Bologna stakeholders support Germany in leading the European region in their stability-seeking process, while relying on the EHEA as a platform for this. This resonates well with the literature on the Franco-German relationship in leading the EU and Europeanisation beyond EU's borders (e.g. Krotz & Schramm, 2022; Steible et al., 2022). This relationship is quite close despite some significant differences in their approaches and the resulting tensions, such as in viewing the role of NATO (Major, 2021) or Germany's and EU's questioning the continuity of this influencing power-sharing between Germany and France following the 2024 European Parliament election. The election saw the victory for Macron's rival Marine Le Pen's far-right National Rally party. Although this party did not win the majority in the follow-up snap legislative election in France, the aftershock is palpable of the 'political earthquake' that the unplanned national election has caused and resulted in Macron's centrist coalition coming in second, giving way to the left-wing party New Popular Front coalition to come in first (Chabal & Behrent, 2024, p. 330). The resultant uncertainty leads Macron not to appoint a left-wing Prime Minister following the election (Chabal & Behrent, 2024).

Unlike German and French Bologna stakeholders that were interviewed, Chapter 6 demonstrated that Italian Bologna stakeholders, despite taking a notably coordinating role in the EHEA, have been trying to explore if there was a way not to engage in wider political decisions in the framework of their work in the EHEA, such as not reacting officially to the atrocities in Belarus and the invasion of Ukraine. Such aspirations could be attributed to a few inherent conflicts in Italian recent politics, such as being part of the EU while experiencing growing Euroscepticism (e.g. Pasquinucci, 2022; Zulianello, 2022), advancing these Eurosceptic and other far-right ideas while admitting unity with most of the EU in condemning the Russian aggression against Ukraine (Guerra, 2023). This contextual landscape in Italy and the unavoidable political nature of HE and cooperation in it (Marshall & Scribner, 1991) explains why Italian Bologna stakeholders may have first experienced certain reservations about signing off any declarations of reactions to events abroad in their capacity as Bologna stakeholders, but eventually yielded to the need to do that, given the inseparability of their work in HE and external relations in other policy areas.

Finally, the UK case stands out due to its uniqueness in comparison to the other three cases. Specifically, it has got two members which are represented in the EHEA, namely EWNI and Scotland. These have diverging agendas for their relations with the rest of Europe. In addition, EWNI's and Scotland's motivations for maintaining their EHEA memberships are more self-oriented as compared to the aspirations of Germany, France and Italy to be leaders of some form (albeit different, as explained above) in the European region and its HE space. In EWNI, England's EHEA stakeholders take a leading position in the work of EWNI as a member of the EHEA (Kushnir & Brooks, 2022; Kushnir, 2023). The main objective of these stakeholders has been keeping track of EHEA's developments and wider politics surrounding them, meaning established cooperation ties in the area of HE and seeking ways for expanding this cooperation with other regions, while not being an active leader in the EHEA, let alone the European project. The attitude of EWNI to the Europeanisation politics, arguably, borrows its tone from England's imperial past. For Scotland – the United Kingdom's other EHEA member – HE cooperation in the EHEA is a valuable tool for facilitating

Scotland's persistence on the politics of Europeanisation, particularly in the context of Scotland aiming to improve the shaken relationship with the EU after Brexit (Tilley & Hobolt, 2024; Wright, 2018).

These findings address the first of the three major overlapping gaps in prior scholarship on European HE and European politics – the lack of knowledge about the four founders of the EHEA, particularly the interconnectedness of their EHEA membership agendas and their wider political agendas. Prior literature on the topic included a plethora of single-country studies (e.g. Chies et al., 2019) or collective case studies which never involved data from all four EHEA's founders (e.g. Marquand & Scott, 2018). The primary focus of earlier studies was on the evaluation of Bologna implementation (e.g. Antoniolli, 2006; Field, 2005; Guth, 2006; Malan, 2004). More recent studies (e.g. Kushnir, 2023, 2025; Kushnir & Yazgan, 2023; Marquand & Scott, 2018) have been more diverse in their foci; however, they have not focused on EHEA's founders jointly as a stepping stone for the analysis of European politics. An exception is my recent co-authored article (Kushnir & Yazgan, 2024) which is informed by this same project and represents its extract, analysing the geopolitics of the European HE space. The collective case study of the strategic significance of continuing work in the framework of the EHEA by the four EHEA founders, presented in this book, makes an important contribution to the literature on European HE and European politics. The collective case study covered in this book advances our limited and previously fragmented knowledge about EHEA's initiators, which started to be developed in my earlier articles which presented other smaller aspects of EHEA founders' work and politics (Kushnir & Brooks, 2022; Kushnir, 2023, 2025; Kushnir & Yazgan, 2023, 2024).

Understanding these developments in the four EHEA founders also sheds more light on differentiation in European politics – different degrees of involvement in European policies and various motivations and forms of engagement in European political matters. Literature on this differentiation is vast, including two related large bodies of research on differentiated EU integration (e.g. de Blok et al., 2024; Princen et al., 2024) and differentiated EU policy implementation (e.g. Zhelyazkova et al., 2024), as well as studies discussing the prospects of further EU enlargement (e.g. Kushnir et al., 2020) and differentiated Europeanisation outside the EU (e.g. Fromage, 2024). While the concept 'differentiated Europeanisation', clearly, has its roots in the EU studies, it has also been applied to the analysis of the developments of a much wider area than the EU – the EHEA (Kushnir & Brooks, 2022; Veiga, 2023; Veiga et al., 2015). However, those articles have not focused on the four founding countries of the EHEA in the current climate. The HE perspective on this differentiation is important to inform policymaking on the international level of the EHEA as we are approaching EHEA's 2030 deadline as well as further work of the European Commission and its partners in chairing the development of the European project.

Discussing the gaps in prior scholarship on European HE and European politics cannot take place without the analysis of the link between the two areas – on one hand, European HE, and on the other hand, European politics. This is precisely what the next section focuses on.

8.3 The European Higher Education Area and the European Project

This section builds on the integrated findings from Chapters 4–7 presented above and furthers that discussion to answer the second specific research question that this book has set out to answer – about how these findings inform our understanding of the European project's evolving mission.

The findings from the four founding countries of the EHEA suggest that their stakeholders, despite having different priorities and visions for their memberships in the EHEA and EHEA's role for the European region, have all been contributing to the meaning-making with regard to the purpose of the European project. Given EHEA's role in expanding the borders of Europe (Kushnir, 2016) as well as EU's enlargement and wider cooperation politics in the region (Kushnir et al., 2020), the European project, originally associated mainly with the EU (Rigney, 2012), has, arguably, been surpassing EU's borders. While the EHEA is the largest HE cooperation initiative not only in Europe but in the world (Zahavi & Friedman, 2019a, 2019b), which has penetrated other frameworks such as HE initiatives within the European Education Area (Kushnir, 2021, 2022), it is, evidently, not the only HE cooperation framework. In the area of quality assurance, for instance, a move from the EHEA being 'the near singular focus for European level coordination and harmonisation' to a 'much more diverse and complex quality assurance and evaluation infrastructure' has been taking place (Grek & Russell, 2023, p. 1). The EHEA is, thus, viewed here as an example of European cooperation in HE. The findings presented in this book have demonstrated that the EHEA has emerged as an instrumental platform for the meaning-making process of the European project's mission which has increasingly been gaining momentum in supporting political stability and a cross-country dialogue in the European region, particularly recently – in the early 2020s.

Historical NI prompts the consideration of the fact that there has been no consensus around what Europe is and what it means to be European (Dale & Robertson, 2009; Datler et al., 2021). The debates about Europe's borders (Bellier & Wilson, 2020; Kočan, 2023) have been developing hand in hand with the debates around Europe being a space of meaning (Abélès, 2020; Lawn & Grek, 2012) in its effort to combine unity and diversity among its peoples (Derrida, 1992; Sassatelli, 2021) and to establish its purpose.

As detailed in Chapter 3, the establishment of the EU in 1993 was a milestone in consolidating Europe around a common ideal of post-war peace-keeping and ensuring security on the continent in the face of the collapse of the Soviet Union and Yugoslavia in 1991 (Bebler, 2013; Dedman, 2009). Crucially, however, generation change over time has diminished the initial sense of urgency and need for the post-war peace-building embodied in the development of the European project. Younger people could not relate to those old ideas, and EU's bureaucracy was a drawback the new generations saw in the work of the EU (Polyakova, 2016). Furthermore, new problems such as dealing with forced migration and economic crises became associated with the negatives of being part of the EU (Taggart & Szczerbiak, 2018). This, in turn, propelled populist gains across

European countries (Schraff & Pontusson, 2024). It is helpful to appeal to the sociological NI strand and its emphasis on the role of individuals in organisational change to understand the role of far-right leaders in different European countries who managed to consolidate populist supporters.

The quest to find a more relevant purpose of continuing developing the European project – the EU and its cooperation with the countries around it – went on, and education has emerged as an instrument for facilitating unity. For example, the so-called European dimension has been part of the EHEA from its outset (Kushnir, 2016) and the recent establishment of the European Education Area to aid the deepening of the relationships among the EU Member States (Kushnir, 2021) has signified EU's 'renewed state-making ambitions' (Robertson et al., 2022, p. 65). HE in particular has played an important role in developing the European project through the promotion of academic mobility, facilitating the creation of a European single market and the idea and image of the European citizen (Corbett, 2005; Robertson et al., 2016). Such a key role of education in Europe has been instrumental but it was not as uniting as the post-war peace-building ideal that originally propelled the establishment of the EU. The ideas of unity around peace-building/keeping and (higher) education opportunities for all are of a different nature by default. Thus, expecting them to be mutually replaceable would be naïve. While the EHEA and recently the European Education Area have consolidated the people of the European region around the attractive goal to facilitate cultural exchange and unity as well as social mobility on the continent (Kushnir, 2021), the unplugged void of what exactly Europe is about after the shared understanding of post-WWII peace-building goals have faded (Polyakova, 2016) has been growing.

Brexit which has shaken the stability of the EU, and the full-scale Russian attack on Ukraine – first war of this scale in the Europe region after WWII – has, arguably, changed the dynamics of Europe's ongoing mission (re)establishment process – in line with the logic of historical NI. As demonstrated by some of the findings in Chapters 4–6, these events have reinvigorated the old sentiments of security and war threats and the importance of staying united in facilitating security and peace. What is crucial is that HE seems to have played an important role in addition to such key policy areas in Europe as defence, economy and food security (Ash, 2023; Guerra, 2023). The porousness of Europe's borders has been apparent in Europe's facilitating of security and peace in the European region as the EU has been a key player in this process, acknowledging that the war in Ukraine has actually been taking place in Europe (Ash, 2023).

Evidently, the strategic significance of continuing memberships of Germany, France, Italy and the United Kingdom in the EHEA for them separately as well as the European region in general, summarised earlier in this chapter, informs our understanding of the EHEA serving not only as a platform for HE cooperation but also a political platform for promoting inter-country friendships and stability in the region. Thus, the HE cooperation, illustrated by the case of the EHEA, becomes a symbolic tool for facilitating the politics of friendship in Europe.

This is particularly important now, after 2020, given the main recent milestone in the development of the EHEA in 2020 (EHEA, 2024), which also coincided with a couple of other significant events in European geopolitics such as the end of the Brexit transitional period and the start of a full-scale Russia–Ukraine war. This book has embraced the novelty of this recent multifaceted temporal dimension of the perspectives of key HE actors in EHEA's founding countries on the strategic significance of their memberships in this Area for them, as well as for the European region. This temporal focus of the book has addressed the second of the three major gaps in prior scholarship on European HE and European politics. This has been a gap for three main reasons. First, while many scholars, particularly those interested in UK HE, have discussed HE and Brexit (e.g. Brooks, 2021a, 2021b; Ploner & Nada, 2019; Zotti, 2021), their analysis was not presented as a context specifically for the debates about the EHEA or membership in it. Exceptions include Morgan (2022, p. 124) who speculates that Welsh usage of EHEA's European Credit Transfer System (ECTS) is 'under severe strain as the consequences of Brexit roll out'; however, it is not clear why, as the United Kingdom remains in the EHEA despite exiting the EU and Erasmus+ (Kushnir, 2023; Kushnir & Brooks, 2022). Aside from this, it is also worth noting that Veiga's (2023) reflective piece analyses the EHEA in the context of Brexit but not specifically in the timeframe after the 2020, EHEA's deadline and the war context in Ukraine, and does not look at the stakeholders' view from EHEA's founders. Second, the originality of the temporal focus of this book also lies in contextualising the main focus of the book in terms of the war in Ukraine which is the war in geographical Europe. EHEA's response to the attack on Ukraine has so far been the focus of an article that came out from the same project that has informed this book (Kushnir, 2025). Finally, EHEA's developments after its 2020 deadline have not been reviewed by other scholars. Those who did acknowledge the deadline anticipated the end of work on the EHEA (Gareis & Broekel, 2022; Mendick & Peters, 2022; Pires Pereira et al., 2023).

It is also worth summarising the importance of the foundation that the NI approach has provided in the theorisation of the role of European cooperation in HE in the evolving mission of the European project. Borrowing the insights for this analysis from NI has also contributed to the addressing of the third major gap in the scholarship on European HE and Europeanisation – the lack of application of this approach to the issue in focus. NI serves as a theoretical frame here, given its focus on (formal) institutions (such as the EHEA) that 'operate and develop mobilities, collaborations, interdependencies and interrelationships between central and state institutions, in shaping the right climate for transactions and policy development' (Liargovas & Papageorgiou, 2024, p. 13).

While the rational-choice strand of NI has been key, the other three strands – historical, sociological and discursive – have all played an important role in informing the analysis in this book. The rational-choice strand has allowed to explore the strategic importance of the memberships of the four founders in the EHEA for them and for the European region. This was studied through the voices from key organisations related to the implementation of the Bologna Process in the four founding countries. This focus on strategising behind continuing EHEA memberships also took into account the unavoidably bounded nature of the rational choices of policy actors (Simon, 1990). The analysis has uncovered what was possible in the rational decisions that have been made by these policy actors.

Additionally, the historical strand of NI has informed our understanding of some of these rationalisations, relying on the idea of path-dependency in these decisions and their related developments. Sociological NI was also key in emphasising the role that individuals play in shaping organisational responses (Peters, 2019), particularly with regard to the voices from the organisations represented in the interview sample. Discursive NI, which strongly overlaps with the above three strands, has also been handy in recognising that the discourses of these organisations, represented in the official communications and, in part, in the interviews, shape the essence of the processes that have been analysed.

8.4 Conclusion

This chapter has integrated and further discussed the findings presented in the earlier chapters in light of the theoretical and empirical literature outlined elsewhere in this book. This integrated discussion has answered the key research questions that this book has set out in the beginning and consolidated key aspects of the main argument of the book. The following and final chapter offers final concluding remarks.

References

Abélès, M. (2020). Virtual Europe. In I. Bellier & T. M. Wilson (Eds.), *An anthropology of the European Union* (pp. 31–52). Routledge.

Antoniolli, L. (2006). Legal education in Italy and the Bologna Process. *European Journal of Legal Education, 3*(2), 143–145.

Ash, T. G. (2023). Postimperial empire: How the war in Ukraine is transforming Europe. *Foreign Affairs, 102*, 64.

Bebler, A. (2013). Peace in Europe and the Nobel Peace Prize. *Israel Journal of Foreign Affairs, 7*(3), 115–125. https://doi.org/10.1080/23739770.2013.11446571

Bellier, I., & Wilson, T. M. (2020). Building, imagining and experiencing Europe: Institutions and identities in the European Union. In I. Bellier & T. M. Wilson (Eds.), *An anthropology of the European Union* (pp. 1–27). Routledge.

Bergan, S., & Matei, L. (2020). The future of the Bologna Process and the European Higher Education Area: New perspectives on a recurring topic. In A. Curaj, L. Deca, & R. Pricopie (Eds.), *European higher education area: Challenges for a new decade* (pp. 361–373). Springer International Publishing.

Brooks, R. (2021a). Europe as spatial imaginary? Narratives from higher education 'policy influencers' across the continent. *Journal of Education Policy, 36*(2), 159–178.

Brooks, R. (2021b). The construction of higher education students within national policy: A cross-European comparison. *Compare: A Journal of Comparative and International Education, 51*, 161–180.

Caporaso, J. A. (2021). Germany and the eurozone crisis: Power, dominance, and hegemony. In M. Kim & J. Caporaso (Eds.), *Power relations and comparative regionalism* (pp. 18–43). Routledge.

Chabal, E., & Behrent, M. C. (2024). The deluge: France's 2024 legislative elections. *Modern & Contemporary France*, *32*(3), 329–337. https://doi.org/10.1080/09639489. 2024.2381787

Chies, L., Graziosi, G., & Pauli, F. (2019). The impact of the Bologna Process on graduation: New evidence from Italy. *Research in Higher Education*, *60*, 203–218. https://doi.org/10.1007/s11162-018-9512-4

Corbett, A. (2005). *Universities and the Europe of knowledge – Ideas, institutions and policy entrepreneurship in European Union higher education policy, 1955–2005*. Palgrave Macmillan. https://doi.org/10.1057/9780230286467

Dale, R., & Robertson, S. (2009). *Globalisation and Europeanisation in Education*. Symposium Books.

Datler, G., Roessel, J., & Schroedter, J. H. (2021). What is Europe? The meaning of Europe in different social contexts in Switzerland. *Swiss Political Science Review*, *27*(2), 390–411.

de Blok, L., Heermann, M., Schuessler, J., Leuffen, D., & de Vries, C. E. (2024). All on board? The role of institutional design for public support for differentiated integration. *European Union Politics*. https://doi.org/10.1177/14651165241246384

Dedman, M. (2009). *The origins & development of the European Union 1945-2008: A history of European integration*. Routledge. https://doi.org/10.4324/9780203873618

Derrida, J. (1992). *The other heading: Reflections on today's Europe*. Indiana University Press.

EHEA. (2020). Rome Ministerial Communique. https://ehea.info/Upload/Rome_Ministerial_Communique.pdf. Accessed on February 10, 2025.

EHEA. (2024). How does the Bologna Process work? https://www.ehea.info/page-how-does-the-bologna-process-work. Accessed on June 10, 2024.

Field, J. (2005). Bologna and an established system of bachelor's/master's degrees: The example of adult education in Britain. *Bildung und Erziehung*, *58*(2), 207–220.

Fromage, D. (2024). *Redefining EU membership: differentiation in and outside the European Union*. Oxford University Press.

Gareis, P., & Broekel, T. (2022). The spatial patterns of student mobility before, during and after the Bologna Process in Germany. *Tijdschrift voor Economische en Sociale Geografie*, *113*(3), 290–309. https://doi.org/10.1111/tesg.12507

Grek, S., & Russell, I. (2023). Beyond Bologna? Infrastructuring quality in European higher education. *European Educational Research Journal*, 1–22. https://doi.org/10.1177/14749041231170518

Guerra, N. (2023). The Russia-Ukraine war has shattered the Italian far right. *Behavioral Sciences of Terrorism and Political Aggression*, 1–21. https://doi.org/10.1080/19434472.2023.2206468

Guth, J. (2006). The bologna process: The impact of higher education reform on the structure and organisation of doctoral programmes in Germany. *Higher Education in Europe*, *31*(3), 327–338.

Kočan, F. (2023). Europeanisation, securitisation and ontological insecurity. In *Identity, ontological security and Europeanisation in Republika Srpska* (pp. 13–72). Springer Nature Switzerland.

Krotz, U., & Schramm, L. (2022). Embedded bilateralism, integration theory, and European crisis politics: France, Germany, and the birth of the EU corona recovery fund. *JCMS: Journal of Common Market Studies*, *60*(3), 526–544. https://doi.org/10.1111/jcms.13211

Kushnir, I. (2016). The role of the Bologna Process in defining Europe. *European Educational Research Journal*, *15*(6), 664–675. https://doi.org/10.1177/1474904116657549

Kushnir, I. (2021). The role of the European Education Area in European Union integration in times of crises. *European Review*, *30*(3), 301–321. https://doi.org/10.1017/S1062798721000016

Kushnir, I. (2022). Referentiality mechanisms in EU education policymaking: The case of the European Education Area. *European Journal of Education*. https://doi.org/10.1111/ejed.12485

Kushnir, I. (2023). Rational-choice neo-institutionalism in Europeanization in the UK and Germany: A toolkit offered by their memberships in the European Higher Education Area. *European Education*, *55*(2), 61–77.

Kushnir, I. (2025). 'It is more than just education. It's also a peace policy': (Re)imagining the mission of the European Higher Education Area in the context of the Russian invasion of Ukraine. *European Educational Research Journal*, *24*(1), 111–126.

Kushnir, I., & Brooks, R. (2022). UK membership(s) in the European Higher Education Area post-2020: A 'Europeanisation' agenda. *European Educational Research Journal*. https://doi.org/10.1177/14749041221083

Kushnir, I., Kilkey, M., & Strumia, F. (2020). EU integration in the (post)-migrant-crisis context: Learning new integration modes? *European Review*, *28*(2), 306–324.

Kushnir, I., & Yazgan, N. (2023). The politics of higher education: The European Higher Education Area through the eyes of its stakeholders in France and Italy. *Humanities and Social Sciences Communications*, *10*, 774.

Kushnir, I., & Yazgan, N. (2024). Shifting geopolitics of the European higher education space. *European Journal of Higher Education*, 1–22.

Lawn, M., & Grek, S. (2012). *Europeanising education: Governing a new policy space*. Symposium Books. https://doi.org/10.15730/books.78

Liargovas, P., & Papageorgiou, C. (Eds.). (2024). Theoretical perspectives on European integration and its evolutionary trajectory. In *The European integration, Vol. 2: Institutions and policies* (pp. 11–55). Springer Nature Switzerland.

Major, C. (2021). A Committed but challenging ally: France's NATO policy. In R. Kempin (Ed.), *France's foreign and security policy under president Macron: The consequences for Franco-German cooperation*. SWP Research Paper. https://doi.org/10.18449/2021RP04

Malan, T. (2004). Implementing the Bologna Process in France. *European Journal of Education*, *39*(3), 289–297.

Marquand, J., & Scott, P. (Eds.). (2018). United Kingdom: England (and Wales up to 1999) – Aesop's hare. In *Democrats, authoritarians and the Bologna process* (pp. 127–161). Emerald Publishing Limited.

Marshall, C., & Scribner, J. D. (1991). "It's all political" inquiry into the micropolitics of education. *Education and Urban Society*, *23*(4), 347–355. https://doi.org/10.1177/0013124591023004001

Mendick, H., & Peters, A. K. (2022). How post-Bologna policies construct the purposes of higher education and students' transitions into Masters programmes. *European Educational Research Journal*, *22*(2). https://doi.org/10.1177/14749041221076633

Morgan, B. (2022). Credit and curriculum in Wales, devolution, Bologna and Brexit: An eclectic journey. In L. Thomas (Ed.), *Widening access to higher education in the UK: Developments and approaches using credit accumulation and transfer* (p. 110). Routledge.

Pasquinucci, D. (2022). From narrative to counter-narrative: The European constraint and the rise of Italian populist Euroscepticism. *Journal of Contemporary European Studies, 30*(1), 39–51. https://doi.org/10.1080/14782804.2020.1839396

Peters, B. (2019). *Institutional theory in political science: The new institutionalism.* Edward Elgar Publishing.

Pires Pereira, I.S., Fernandes, E. L., Braga, A. C., & Flores, M. A. (2023). Initial teacher education after the Bologna Process. Possibilities and challenges for a renewed scholarship of teaching and learning. *European Journal of Teacher Education, 46*(2), 1–29. https://doi.org/10.1080/02619768.2020.1867977

Ploner, J., & Nada, C. (2019). International student migration and the postcolonial heritage of European higher education: Perspectives from Portugal and the UK. *Higher Education, 80,* 373–389.

Polyakova, A. (2016). The great European unravelling? *World Policy Journal, 33*(4), 68–72. https://doi.org/10.1215/07402775-3813051

Princen, S., Schimmelfennig, F., Sczepanski, R., Smekal, H., & Zbiral, R. (2024). Different yet the same? Differentiated integration and flexibility in implementation in the European Union. *West European Politics, 47*(3), 466–490.

Rigney, A. (2012). Transforming memory and the European project. *New Literary History, 43*(4), 607–628.

Robertson, S., de Azevedo, M., & Dale, R. (2016). Higher education, the EU and the cultural political economy of regionalism. In S. L. Robertson, K. Olds, R. Dale, & Q. A. Dang (Eds.), *Global regionalisms and higher education* (pp. 24–48). Edward Elgar Publishing.

Robertson, S. L., Olds, K., & Dale, R. (2022). From the EHEA to the EEA: Renewed state-making ambitions in the regional governance of education in Europe. In M. Klemenčič (Ed.), *From actors to reforms in European higher education: A festschrift for Pavel Zgaga* (pp. 65–76). Springer International Publishing. https://doi.org/10.1007/978-3-031-09400-2

Sassatelli, M. (2021). Europe's cosmopolitan identity. Images of unity in diversity in the euro. In F. Mangiapane & T. Migliore (Eds.), *Images of Europe: The union between federation and separation* (pp. 195–208). Springer International Publishing.

Schraff, D., & Pontusson, J. (2024). Falling behind whom? Economic geographies of right-wing populism in Europe. *Journal of European Public Policy, 31*(6), 1591–1619.

Simon, H. A. (1990). Bounded rationality. In J. Eatwell, M. Milgate, & P. Newman (Eds.), *Utility and probability* (pp. 15–18). Palgrave Macmillan. https://doi.org/10.1007/978-1-349-20568-4

Steible, B., Ramiro Troitiño, D. R., Martín de la Guardia, R., & Pérez Sánchez, G. A. (2022). Emmanuel Macron: The return of France as a driving force for European integration? *The European Union and its political leaders: Understanding the integration process* (pp. 279–294). Springer International Publishing.

Taggart, P., & Szczerbiak, A. (2018). Putting Brexit into perspective: The effect of the Eurozone and migration crises and Brexit on Euroscepticism in European states.

Journal of European Public Policy, 25(8), 1194–1214. https://doi.org/10.1080/13501763.2018.1467955

Tilley, J., & Hobolt, S. B. (2024). Losers' consent and emotions in the aftermath of the Brexit referendum. *West European Politics, 47*(5), 1180–1198.

Veiga, A. (2023). Unthinking the European Higher Education Area: Differentiated integration and Bologna's different configurations. In C. Dienel (Ed.), *Globalizing higher education and strengthening the European spirit* (pp. 93–110). Routledge.

Veiga, A., Magalhaes, A., & Amaral, A. (2015). Differentiated integration and the Bologna Process. *Journal of Contemporary European Research, 11*(1), 84–102.

Wright, A. (Ed.). (2018). Scotland and the EU: All bark and no bite? In *Scotland: The challenge of devolution* (pp. 151–163). Routledge.

Zahavi, H., & Friedman, Y. (2019a). The Bologna Process: An international higher education regime. *European Journal of Higher Education, 9*(1), 23–39. https://doi.org/10.1080/21568235.2018.1561314

Zahavi, H., & Friedman, Y. (2019b). The Bologna Process: An international higher education regime. *European Journal of Higher Education, 9*(1), 23–39. https://doi.org/10.1080/21568235.2018.1561314

Zhelyazkova, A., Thomann, E., Ruffing, E., & Princen, S. (2024). Differentiated policy implementation in the European Union. *West European Politics, 47*(3), 439–465.

Zotti, S. (2021). Academic mobility after Brexit: Erasmus and the UK post-2020. *European Journal of English Studies, 25*(1), 19–33.

Zulianello, M. (2022). Italian general election 2022: The populist radical right goes mainstream. *Political Insight, 13*(4), 20–23.

Chapter 9

Conclusion

Authored by Iryna Kushnir

Abstract

This is the final chapter of this book, which summarises the story in the book and its contributions. This chapter also proposes further research directions that stem from the research findings presented in the earlier chapters.

Keywords: Higher education; European Higher Education Area; EHEA; European project; Europe

This book has presented a collective case study of the four European Higher Education Area's (EHEA) founders' perspectives on the role of the EHEA, viewed as a case of European cooperation in higher education (HE), in understanding the evolving mission of the European project, that has increasingly been transcending the borders of the European Union (EU). The temporal focus covered the early 2020s (data collection finished in 2022 but the analysis also considered political developments in the European region up to mid-2024).

This exploration was framed by the neo-institutionalist approach. In brief, neo-institutionalism enables the analysis of organisational behaviour by focusing on how organisations (or in other terms – institutions), both formal and informal, interact among one another and with a wider society and, more importantly, how organisations change under the influence of wider processes – contextual factors that influence these organisations and are, in turn, influenced by them (Peters, 2019). In this book, both the EHEA itself (as well as its stakeholders on the national level of the signatory countries) and the European project have been viewed as organisations, albeit, understandably, of a different nature. There are four key interconnected strands of neo-institutionalism: historical, sociological, rational choice (Peters, 2019) and discursive neo-institutionalism (Schmidt, 2014).

All the strands consider institutions as the main variable in analysing phenomena related to politics.

A thematic analysis of 25 interviews with major HE actors in the four EHEA's founders (Germany $n = 8$, France $n = 4$, Italy $n = 7$, UK $n = 6$) and the analysis of 64 official communications, most of which were produced by these key actors between 2016 and 2022, generated important timely and original findings. Based on these findings, this study contributes to literature and informs policy practice.

The analysis in the previous chapters has demonstrated that European cooperation in HE, exemplified by the EHEA, has been a platform for the meaning-making process of the European project's mission which has been gaining momentum in supporting political stability in the European region, predominantly recently – in the early 2020s. The findings presented in this book suggest that the stakeholders of each of the EHEA's founding countries (i.e. Germany, France, Italy and the United Kingdom), despite having different priorities and visions for their memberships in the EHEA and EHEA's role for Europe, have all been contributory to the making of the purpose of the European project as an insurer of stability and dialogue among the countries.

More specifically, Germany's EHEA membership is viewed by Germany's Bologna stakeholders largely as a tool for generating and maintaining political stability in the European region, and Germany is an active leader in this process. France's Bologna stakeholders have taken more of a moderating role in the leading process of the European region, together with Germany. In their stability-seeking process, the Bologna stakeholders of both France and Germany rely on the EHEA as a key platform. Aside from this, Italian Bologna stakeholders, despite taking an important coordinating role in the EHEA, have been trying to stay apolitical before succumbing to the unavoidable connection between politics and HE. This behaviour may, arguably, stem from the inherent contradiction in the Italy's attempts to combine its continuing EHEA membership, linked to Europeanisation (Kushnir, 2021), and Italy's increasing Euroscepticism, coupled with Italy's ongoing commitment to the security of the region (Zulianello, 2022). A similar conflict seems to be present in the attitude of England, Wales and N.Ireland (EWNI) – one of the two UK members in the EHEA, along with Scotland which is the other UK member in the EHEA. However, this conflict is expressed differently in EWNI's positioning of its EHEA membership. EWNI, where England's Bologna stakeholders lead relevant work (Kushnir & Brooks, 2022), have been observing EHEA developments and wider politics around it, maintaining the established cooperation ties in the area of HE with other countries in the EHEA but looking outwards to establish similar ties with other regions. For Scotland, HE cooperation in the framework of the EHEA is a platform to extend the politics of Europeanisation, shaken after Brexit.

The research spelled out in this book *contributes*, first and foremost, to the body of literature that investigates European HE and European politics as there has been a lack of knowledge about the four founders of the EHEA, and particularly the interconnectedness of their EHEA membership agendas and their wider political agendas. Previous research on this topic comprises a lot of single-country studies (e.g. Chies et al., 2019) and collective case studies

Conclusion   123

(e.g. Marquand & Scott, 2018), but they lack data from all four EHEA's founding countries. The main focus of many earlier studies was on evaluating the implementation of the Bologna Process (BP) in the given countries (e.g Antoniolli, 2006; Field, 2005; Guth, 2006; Malan, 2004). The foci of recent studies (e.g. Kushnir, 2023; Kushnir & Yazgan, 2023; Marquand & Scott, 2018) are more varied but they have not explored EHEA's founders jointly as a case for informing our understanding of European politics. One exception is my recent co-authored article (Kushnir & Yazgan, 2024) which analyses the geopolitics of the European HE space, but it came out from this same project and represents its extract. This collective case study of the strategic significance of continuing work in the framework of the EHEA by the founding countries of the EHEA, presented in this book, makes an important contribution to the scholarship about European HE and European politics. This book advances our fragmented knowledge about EHEA's founders, which started to be pieced together in my earlier articles (Kushnir & Brooks, 2022; Kushnir, 2023, 2025; Kushnir & Yazgan, 2023, 2024).

Second, the study reported here addresses a temporal-contextual gap in the available field of research on the EHEA by covering the current period – early 2020s – namely after the main recent milestone in the development of the EHEA in 2020 (EHEA, 2024b), which also coincided with a couple of other significant events in European geopolitics, such as the end of the Brexit transitional period and the start of a full-scale Russia–Ukraine war. This temporal focus has been an under-researched gap in prior scholarship on European HE and European politics. While many researchers, especially those exploring UK HE, have analysed HE and Brexit (e.g. Ploner & Nada, 2019; Zotti, 2021), their works did not aim to serve as a context specifically for the discussion of the EHEA. There are, of course, a couple of exceptions. For example, Veiga's (2023) reflective piece discusses the EHEA in the Brexit context but not specifically after EHEA's 2020 deadline and the war context in Ukraine, neither does it research the stakeholders' view from EHEA's founders. Aside from this, EHEA's post-2020 developments have not been investigated in prior related research. Those who acknowledged EHEA's 2020 deadline did so with the apparent anticipation of the end of the work on the EHEA in 2020 (e.g. Gareis & Broekel, 2022; Mendick & Peters, 2022; Pires Pereira et al., 2021).

Third, this book has highlighted an innovative theoretical dimension in the topic European HE and European politics by relying on neo-institutionalism. Borrowing the insights from the four strands of neo-institutionalism for the analysis of the role of European cooperation in HE in the evolving mission of the European project has also contributed to the addressing of the third major gap in the scholarship on European HE and Europeanisation. There is a lack of application of neo-institutionalism in this area. The rational-choice strand has been key in exploring the strategic importance of the memberships of the four EHEA founders for them and for the European region. This was investigated by relying on the voices from major organisations related to the implementation of the BP in the four countries of interest. The analysis also considered the unavoidably bounded nature of the rational choices of policy actors (Simon, 1990), as it helped to see what was possible in the rational decisions that have been taken by these actors.

In addition, historical neo-institutionalism was key to understanding path dependency in these decisions and any developments that stemmed from them. Aside from this, the key role of individuals in shaping organisational responses was explored with the help of sociological neo-institutionalism (Peters, 2019). This was related to the voices from the organisations represented in the interview sample, in particular. The final strand of neo-institutionalism – discursive neo-institutionalism – overlaps with the other three strands. Discursive neo-institutionalism has been useful in appreciating that the discourses generated and maintained by the organisations, mentioned above, were represented in the data generated by the project – official communications and, partly, the interviews with the representatives from these organisations. These discourses have shaped the essence of the processes at stake.

The findings of the study presented in this book and its limitations, mentioned below, can serve as a stepping stone to *further research* in such three main areas: exploring the perspectives of other EHEA countries on the role of European HE cooperation for the development of Europe, looking in particular at the growing context of far-right movements and related populism and Euroscepticism in Europe with regard to the positioning of the European cooperation in HE as a foundation for the development of Europe; and investigating the reasons and implications for the growing interconnectedness of the EHEA processes with other European HE processes particularly those related to the European Education Area (EEA).

The first area for further investigation is the perspectives of Bologna stakeholders in other EHEA countries on the role of their cooperation in the framework of the EHEA for the European project. This book looked only at four out of the active 47 EHEA signatories, excluding the two suspended members, namely the Russian Federation and Belarus (EHEA, 2024a). These four countries are the founders of the EHEA. However, they do not have any formally allocated more dominant role in leading the EHEA, apart from the established power dynamics where, for example, Germany and France cooperate in leading the European region in general, and Italy coordinating many recent developments in the EHEA, as explained in the earlier chapters. Further research would be beneficial into other EHEA members' perspectives on the role of European cooperation in HE for Europe, particularly the non-EU countries that belong to the EHEA and those traditionally not viewed as European such as Kazakhstan (Kushnir, 2016). Analysing the implications for Europe of not expelling the Russian Foundation and Belarus from the EHEA but rather suspending their memberships is also an interesting angle to the issue at stake. Juxtaposing the findings in this book and those from the suggested further research in this area would shed more light on the relationship between HE cooperation in the framework of the EHEA and the development of the European project.

Besides further investigating the perspectives of other EHEA countries on the role of HE cooperation for Europe, another focus for future related studies should be on the growing context of far-right movements which have been facilitating populism and Euroscepticism in Europe (Schraff & Pontusson, 2024) with regard to the instrumental role of European cooperation in HE for Europe. Data collection for this book finished before such significant political events took place as, for instance, the 2024 European Parliament election featuring far-right gains in France (European Parliament, 2024) and the 2024 snap French legislative election which Macron had hoped would demonstrate strong support for him. Instead, it created a political chaos as while the far-right did not win, Macron's centrist coalition coming in second, giving way to the left-wing party New Popular Front coalition to come in first. The uncertainty brought about by the surprise early election following far-right gains in the European Parliament election has lead Macron not to appoint a left-wing Prime Minister (Chabal & Behrent, 2024). This is an important changing context in Europe, and its relationship to HE should be further explored in next related studies that explore the post-2020 context beyond the early 2020s.

Finally, further research should investigate the reasons and implications for the growing interconnectedness of the EHEA with other European HE processes (Grek & Russell, 2024) particularly those related to the EEA. While the EHEA has been working on (re)establishing its distinctiveness (Kushnir, 2025), the interconnections between the EHEA and specifically some of the EEA processes such as the European universities initiative have been apparent (Kushnir, 2022). Deliberate efforts to do this are, in part, surprising, given the positioning of the establishment of the EEA as a means to deepen the relationships specifically among the EU member states (Kushnir, 2021) which has signified EU's 'renewed state-making ambitions' (Robertson et al., 2022, p. 65). However, it would be naïve to anticipate a complete segregation of the EHEA and EEA initiatives as they do share many commonalities not just in terms of the countries which are their members but also in the nature of the HE cooperation initiatives they promote. While the EEA is briefly discussed in Chapter 3 as part of the context for the focus of this book, the relationship between the EHEA and the EEA was beyond the scope of this study. Yet, this relationship is an important area to investigate in further research to grasp the evolving nuances of the interconnection between HE cooperation initiatives in Europe in continuing exploring their role in the making of Europe.

European cooperation in the area of HE might seem to be a very peculiar case of what shapes and, in turn, reveals the unfolding mission of the European project, which itself by default is always under construction. As this book has demonstrated, not only European cooperation in HE has historically been crucial for the making of Europe, but it has recently played a remarkably important role in uniting the peoples of the European Union and around it in the pursuit of a common goal of building social capital in the region while promoting the interconnectedness and friendships among the countries on various levels. Perhaps, this is precisely the reason that the study of Europeanisation through HE cooperation initiatives is such a promising and productive field of research.

References

Antoniolli, L. (2006). Legal education in Italy and the Bologna Process. *European Journal of Legal Education*, *3*(2), 143–145.

Chabal, E., & Behrent, M. C. (2024). The deluge: France's 2024 legislative elections. *Modern and Contemporary France*, *32*(3), 329–337. https://doi.org/10.1080/09639489.2024.2381787

Chies, L., Graziosi, G., & Pauli, F. (2019). The impact of the Bologna Process on graduation: New evidence from Italy. *Research in Higher Education*, *60*, 203–218. https://doi.org/10.1007/s11162-018-9512-4

EHEA. (2024a). Full members. https://ehea.info/page-full_members. Accessed on August 21, 2024.

EHEA. (2024b). How does the Bologna Process work? https://ehea.info/page-how-does-the-bologna-process-work. Accessed on August 21, 2024.

European Parliament. (2024). European elections 6–9 June 2024. https://elections.europa.eu/en/. Accessed on August 21, 2024.

Field, J. (2005). Bologna and an established system of bachelor's/master's degrees: The example of adult education in Britain. *Bildung und Erziehung*, *58*(2), 207–220.

Gareis, P., & Broekel, T. (2022). The spatial patterns of student mobility before, during and after the Bologna process in Germany. *Tijdschrift voor Economische en Sociale Geografie*, *113*(3), 290–309. https://doi.org/10.1111/tesg.12507

Grek, S., & Russell, I. (2024). Beyond Bologna? Infrastructuring quality in European higher education. *European Educational Research Journal*, *23*(2), 215–236.

Guth, J. (2006). The bologna process: The impact of higher education reform on the structure and organisation of doctoral programmes in Germany. *Higher Education in Europe*, *31*(3), 327–338.

Kushnir, I. (2016). The role of the Bologna Process in defining Europe. *European Educational Research Journal*, *15*(6), 664–675. https://doi.org/10.1177/1474904116657549

Kushnir, I. (2021). The role of the European Education Area in European Union integration in times of crises. *European Review*, *30*(3), 301–321.

Kushnir, I. (2022). Referentiality mechanisms in EU education policymaking: The case of the European education area. *European Journal of Education*, *57*(1), 128–141.

Kushnir, I. (2023). Rational-choice neo-institutionalism in Europeanization in the UK and Germany: A toolkit offered by their memberships in the European Higher Education Area. *European Education*, *55*(2), 61–77.

Kushnir, I. (2025). 'It is more than just education. It's also a peace policy': (Re) imagining the mission of the European Higher Education Area in the context of the Russian invasion of Ukraine. *European Educational Research Journal*, *24*(1), 111–126.

Kushnir, I., & Brooks, R. (2022). UK membership(s) in the European Higher Education Area post-2020: A 'Europeanisation' agenda. *European Educational Research Journal*. https://doi.org/10.1177/14749041221083077

Kushnir, I., & Yazgan, N. (2023). The politics of higher education: The European Higher Education Area through the eyes of its stakeholders in France and Italy. *Humanities and Social Sciences Communications*, *10*, 774.

Kushnir, I., & Yazgan, N. (2024). Shifting geopolitics of the European higher education space. *European Journal of Higher Education*, 1–22.

Malan, T. (2004). Implementing the Bologna Process in France. *European Journal of Education*, *39*(3), 289–297.

Marquand, J., & Scott, P. (2018). United Kingdom: England (and Wales up to 1999)– Aesop's hare. In *Democrats, authoritarians and the Bologna Process* (pp. 127–161). Emerald Publishing Limited.

Mendick, H., & Peters, A. K. (2022). How post-Bologna policies construct the purposes of higher education and students' transitions into masters programmes. *European Educational Research Journal*, *22*(2). https://doi.org/10.1177/14749041221076633

Peters, B. (2019). *Institutional theory in political science: The new institutionalism*. Edward Elgar Publishing. ISBN 9781786437921.

Pires Pereira, Í.S., Fernandes, E. L., Braga, A. C., & Flores, M. A. (2021). Initial teacher education after the Bologna Process. Possibilities and challenges for a renewed scholarship of teaching and learning. *European Journal of Teacher Education*, *46*(2), 1–29. https://doi.org/10.1080/02619768.2020.1867977

Ploner, J., & Nada, C. (2019). International student migration and the postcolonial heritage of European Higher Education: Perspectives from Portugal and the UK. *Higher Education*, *80*(2), 373–389.

Robertson, S. L., Olds, K., & Dale, R. (2022). From the EHEA to the EEA: Renewed state-making ambitions in the regional governance of education in Europe. In M. Klemenčič (Ed.), *From actors to reforms in European higher education: A festschrift for Pavel Zgaga* (pp. 65–76). Springer International Publishing. https://doi.org/10.1007/978-3-031-09400-2

Schmidt, V. A. (2014). Speaking to the markets or to the people? A discursive institutionalist analysis of the EU's sovereign debt crisis. *The British Journal of Politics & International Relations*, *16*(1), 188–209. https://doi.org/10.1111/1467-856X.12023

Schraff, D., & Pontusson, J. (2024). Falling behind whom? Economic geographies of right-wing populism in Europe. *Journal of European Public Policy*, *31*(6), 1591–1619.

Simon, H. A. (1990). Bounded rationality. In J. Eatwell, M. Milgate, & P. Newman (Eds.), *Utility and probability* (pp. 15–18). Palgrave Macmillan. https://doi.org/10.1007/978-1-349-20568-4

Veiga, A. (2023). Unthinking the European Higher Education Area: Differentiated integration and Bologna's different configurations. In *Globalizing higher education and strengthening the European spirit* (pp. 93–110). Routledge.

Zotti, S. (2021). Academic mobility after Brexit: Erasmus and the UK post-2020. *European Journal of English Studies*, *25*(1), 19–33.

Zulianello, M. (2022). Italian general election 2022: The populist radical right goes mainstream. *Political Insight*, *13*(4), 20–23.

Index

Actors, 20
Advocacy Coalition Framework, 18–19
Agenzia Nationale di Valutazione del Sistema Universitario e della Ricerca (ANVUR), 77–78
Alternative for Germany Party (AfD), 47
América Latina–Formacíon Acadéмica programme (ALFA programme), 36
Americanisation, 36
Apoliticism
    coordinating role of Italy's membership in EHEA and politics of attempted, 79–83
    paradoxes in Italy's driving EHEA, 81–83
Assembly of Directors of University Institutes of Technology (ADIUT), 58, 64–66

Behavioural choice movements, 19
Belarus politics, 82
Bologna, 10
    action, 38–39
    document, 96–97
    reform, 78
    stakeholders, 6, 9, 22, 45–46, 49, 51, 66, 90, 110
Bologna Follow Up Group (BFUG), 82
Bologna Process (BP), 2, 25, 33, 36–38, 46, 58, 74, 91, 93–95, 114–115, 122–123
    in France, 63–64
    in Germany, 48
    in Italy, 77–79
Borders, 32

Bounded rationality idea, 24
Brexit vote, 10, 92–93
Business, Law and Social Sciences Research Ethics Committee (BLSS REC), 6

Change of European geopolitics, 32
Comitato Nazionale la valutazione del sistema universitario (CNVSU), 77–78
Common Asylum System (CAS), 34
Communicative discourse, 23
Conference of Italian University Rectors (CRUI), 74, 79
Context, 34
Continuing Policy Journey, 109
Coordinative discourse, 23
COVID-19
    crisis, 59–62
    pandemic, 58–59, 62, 66, 77, 93
    safety, 59
    vaccine, 59
Critical junctures, 21
Criticism, 23–24, 26

Data collection, 6
Decision-making, 80–81
Deep-rooted bilateral relationship, 60
Democracy, 80
Democratic party (PD), 76
Differentiated Europeanisation, 4, 111
Discursive neo-institutionalism, 124
Discursive strand, 23

Education, 50
    policy harmonisation project, 37
    provision, 66
    system, 48, 99–100
Education and Training (ET), 2, 36–37

Index

Election, 75–76, 109–110
Electoral competition, 19
Empirical research, 4
England, Wales and Northern Ireland (EWNI), 6, 89–90, 94, 97, 99, 109, 122
England's Bologna stakeholders, 91
Enthusiasm, 94
Erasmus programmes, 37
Europe, 10, 32, 125
   borders, 112
   Europe, higher education and EHEA, 1–3
   focus and originality of book, 3–6
   indispensable nation, 47
   memberships of United Kingdom, Germany, France and Italy in EHEA, 6
   methodological considerations, 6–13
   official communications from national stakeholders, 11
European Commission (EC), 36, 80–81
European Cooperation, 3, 18, 122–125
   EHEA and European project, 112–115
   membership in EHEA, 109–111
European Council, 61–62
European Credit Transfer and Accumulation System (ECTS), 94
European Credit Transfer System (ECTS), 37, 113–114
European cultural integration, 62
European dimension, 113
European education, 35
European Education Area (EEA), 2, 36–37, 65, 113, 124
European financial crisis, 77
European Free Trade Association, 34
European geopolitics, 39, 95, 113–114, 123
European Higher Education and Bologna Process, 82–83
European Higher Education Area (EHEA), 2, 10, 18, 31, 45–46, 57, 73–74, 89–90, 108, 121
   and European project, 112–115
   Europeanisation and internationalisation associated with EHEA in United Kingdom, 101–102
   forum for cooperation in higher education in European region intertwined with wider politics o as f Europe, 79–81
   learning to build, 37–38
   membership in, 109–111
   passive, yet complex, role of United kingdom's memberships in EHEA and politics of Europeanisation and internationalisation, 95–102
   website, 96–97
European identity-seeking process, 33
European Parliament election, 47, 61, 124–125
European politics, 111
   evolution in France and Macron's leadership, 60–61
European project, 1–2, 17–18, 31–32, 35, 108, 113, 121–122
   borders, 32
   European higher education area and, 112–115
   evolving mission of, 34–35
   higher education and, 35–38
   instrumental role of France's membership in EHEA in moderating, 64–67
   learning to build EHEA, 37–38
   role of higher education in Europe historically, 35–37
   space of meaning, 32–33
   unity and diversity, 33–34
European Recovery, 61–62

European region, Germany's membership in EHEA as channel for soft power in promoting stability in, 49–52
European Union (EU), 1–2, 10, 31–32, 46–47, 75, 91, 108, 121, 125
  decision-makers, 2
  Erasmus mobility programme, 35–36
European Universities Initiative, 65
Europeanisation, 1–3, 51, 58, 61, 63–64, 93, 97, 101, 122
  associated with EHEA in UK, 101–102
  passive, yet complex, role of UK memberships in EHEA and politics of, 95–102
  politics, 25–26, 91, 108, 110–111
Eurosceptic views, 91–92
Euroscepticism, 74, 77, 80–81, 124–125

Familiarisation, 13
Fata Morgana, 109
Federal Ministry of Education and Research, 46
Federalism, 17–18
Five Star Movement (M5s), 74–76
Forza Italia (FI), 74–75
France, 2–3, 107–108
  Bologna stakeholders, 65, 122
  BP in France, 63–64
  crises as context, 58–60
  evolution of European politics in France and Macron's leadership, 60–61
  evolution of European politics in France leadership, 60–61
  Franco–German relationship, 61–62
  instrumental role of France's membership in EHEA in moderating European project, 64–67
  leadership, 64
  memberships in European higher education area, 6
  recent developments in French politics, 58–62
Franco-German partnership, 61–62
Franco–German relationship, 61–62
Free Association of Students' Unions (FZS), 46
French
  healthcare system, 60
  HEIs, 63
  leadership, 62
  legislative election, 124–125
  politics, 58
  RN, 58–59
Fuel, 1–2
Functionalism, 17–18

Geopolitics, 111
German Alternative for Germany (AfD), 58–59
German Bologna stakeholders, 46
German politics, 46
Germany, 2–3, 45–46, 49, 107–108
  Bologna stakeholders, 50
  BP in Germany, 48
  effective leadership, 47
  Germany's membership in EHEA as channel for soft power in promoting stability in European region, 49–52
  learning process, 47
  memberships in European higher education area, 6
  recent developments in German politics, 46–47
Global leadership, 47
Global politics, 62
Governance mode, 80
Government official communications, 98–99
Government policies, 58–59
Gradual process, 76

Index

Higher education (HE), 2, 45–46, 57, 73–74, 108, 121
   and European project, 35–38
   Europeanisation, 35–36
   learning to build EHEA, 37–38
   role of higher education in Europe historically, 35–37
Higher education institutions (HEIs), 63
Historical neo-institutionalism, 74, 91, 97
Human rights, 80

Imagined community, 33
Immigration, 46–47, 58–59, 76–77
Immigration policies, 60
In-depth semi-structured elite interviews, 6, 9, 58
Individuals, 21–22
Institutional elements, 25
Institutionalism, 17–18
Institutions, 20
Intergovernmentalism, 17–18
International Education Strategy, 97–98
International higher education regime, 38
Internationalisation, 48
   associated with EHEA in United Kingdom, 101–102
   passive, yet complex, role of UK memberships in EHEA and politics of, 95–102
   process, 102
   strategy, 50
Interviewees, 9–10, 46, 90, 99–100
Interviews, 9, 49, 64, 79
Invasion of Ukraine, 50
Italian Bologna stakeholders, 81
Italian elections, 75–76
Italian membership, 79
Italian recent politics, 110
Italy, 2–3, 107–108
   Bologna process in Italy, 77–79
   coordinating role of Italy's membership in EHEA and politics of attempted apoliticism, 79–83
   EHEA as forum for cooperation in higher education in European region intertwined with wider politics of Europe, 79–81
   memberships in EHEA, 6
   recent developments in Italian politics, 74–77
   traditional two-party system, 74–75

Labour Party, 93
Liberal intergovernmentalism, 17–18
Logic of appropriateness, 22
Lukewarm leadership, 61

Macron's leadership, evolution of European politics in, 60–61
Macron's presidency, 61
Mario Draghi's resignation, 75–76
Meaning-making process, 5, 111
Memberships of United Kingdom, Germany, 6
'Migrant crisis', 33–34
Migration, 92
Ministry of Education, 82
Mission of European project, 34

National official communications, 10
National Report United Kingdom, 97
National Union of Students-UK (NUS-UK), 90
National Union of University Students (UDU), 74
National-level official communications, 10–13
Neofunctionalism, 17–18
Neo–institutionalism (NI), 17–18, 31–32, 39, 46, 80, 108, 121–124
Neo–institutionalist approach, 46, 58, 74, 90

four strands of new institutionalism, 21–23
lens, 39
limitations of new institutionalism, 23–25
locating institutionalist approaches, 18–19
old institutionalism and new institutionalism, 19–20
potential of new institutionalism, 25–26
New institutionalism, 19–20
  discursive strand, 23
  four strands of, 21–23
  historical strand, 21
  limitations of, 23–25
  potential of new institutionalism, 25–26
  rational-choice strand, 22
  sociological strand, 21–22
'New' institutionalist theory, 18

Official communications, 51–52, 64, 79, 122
Old institutionalism, 19–20
Organisational environments, 21–22
Organisations, 20

Paradoxes in Italy's driving EHEA, 81–83
Partito Democraticoarty (PD), 74–75
Path dependency, 21
Peace-building, 1–2, 35
Policy
  discourse, 23
  fragmentation, 48
  implementation, 58–59
  process, 94–95
Policymakers, 22
Political actors, 22
Political behaviour, 21
Political earthquake, 60, 109–110
Political injustice, 81
Political minefield, 92–93
Political organisations, 22
Political science, 19, 25

Politics, 5–6, 81, 91
  passive, yet complex, role of UK memberships in EHEA and politics of Europeanisation and internationalisation, 95–102
Popolo della Libertá (PdL), 74–75
Populism, 75, 124–125
Post-Brexit climate, 67, 95
Post-COVID, 67
Post-war institutions, 2, 35
Postfunctionalism, 17–18
Prior research, understanding gaps in, 38–39
Public policy theories, 18–19

Quality assurance, 78
Quality Assurance Agency, 98–99
Quality Assurance Committee (QAC), 77–78

Rassemblement national (RN), 58–59
Rational choice movements, 19
Rational choice-making process, 98
Rational decision-making, 74
Rational inward-looking approach, 101
Rational-choice strand, 22, 114–115
Rationalisation, 46, 74, 114–115
Reform, 10
Relationship, 125
Republican system, 61
Russian aggression, 46–47
Russia–Ukraine war, 123

Scotland, 99–101
Scottish education system, 96–97
Scottish higher education system, 100
Snap parliamentary elections, 60
Social justice lens, 24
Sociological neo-institutionalism, 124
Sociological strand, 21–22
Soft governance, 48
Space of meaning, 32–33
Stability-seeking process, 5–6, 109–110, 122

Stakeholders, 20
Strategic decisions, 24
Supranationalism, 17–18
Suspending, 82

TEMPUS programmes, 37
Thematic analysis, 49, 122
Three-cycle study system, 63
Transactionalism, 17–18
Transformations, 63

Ukraine, 9, 32, 93
United Kingdom (UK), 2–3, 89–90, 107–108
   and Bologna process, 93–95
   complexity of two memberships, 96–97
   Europeanisation and internationalisation associated with EHEA in UK, 101–102
   EWNI, 97–99
   international student market, 94
   memberships in European higher education area, 6
   passive, yet complex, role of UK memberships in EHEA and politics of Europeanisation and internationalisation, 95–102
   recent developments in, 91–93
   Scotland, 99–101
   split Europeanisation, 91–92
   stakeholders in, 7–8

Vaccination, 59

War
   in European, 2
   on Ukraine, 51

www.ingramcontent.com/pod-product-compliance
Lightning Source LLC
Chambersburg PA
CBHW061942220426
43662CB00012B/1997